ONE COP'S STORY

A Living Testament of God's Grace

Kenneth D. Albright

ONE COP'S STORY

A LIVING TESTAMENT OF GOD'S GRACE
Kenneth D. Albright

First Publication:
Published in the United States of America
Published by
ATC Publishing LLC
P.O. Box 714
Sharpsburg, Georgia 30277
ISBN-13: 978-0692418284
ISBN-10: 0692418288

The events described within this book are factual; however some names have been changed or omitted for the privacy of the individuals or their survivors.

TABLE OF CONTENTS

Nothing Noble is accomplished without Risk, Faith, and Saving Grace from God.

DEDICATION

My heartfelt thanks go out to all of the people that made my life what it is today.

My family, friends and all that I worked with through the years have added something new to who I am.

As I look back over the years, I have no regrets because each step was a learning experience whether good or bad. I had the most wonderful and exciting life that anyone could ask for.

If I had been told as a young man what lay ahead in the next 50 years, I would not have believed that it was possible to have had such a blessed life.

I can only thank God who loves you and me unconditionally.

As mere mortals we may not fully understand and can only believe what He says in His Word, the Living Bible.

A Special Dedication to the Families of those whose lives were lost during my 30 year Career with the Cleveland Police Department.
The 18 Officer's names follow the last chapter.

INTRODUCTION

I have to say I was reluctant to write a book about my police career. My sister had been telling me to write about my adventures on the police department but I felt it was an ego thing and besides, "Who cares about what I did?"

One day I was talking to my pastor about it and he encouraged me to consider it. He said that I had a lot to say, and it wasn't about me but about what God had done in my life.

I respect my pastor's opinion so I started to give it some real thought. The more I thought about it, the more I felt this was something I should do to give God all the glory for what I had accomplished in my life. I could show all the ways He was with me through it all. As I looked back on what I had considered a pretty charmed life, I came to realize that the Lord had been watching over me from day one.

I grew up in the suburbs of Cleveland, Ohio, and had the good fortune of being raised by a Godly mother who loved and served the Lord. I know that she prayed for her four children daily for their salvation and I know God answers prayers. We are living proof of that.

After graduating from high school and after receiving my draft notice in February 1965, I enlisted in the United States Army. During my three year tour, I had the good fortune to travel the world seeing things that I probably would not have been able to on my own. One thing I realize now at this stage of my life, I can look back and see how the Lord had been involved and directed the course of my life. I didn't accept the Lord until the mid-1970s, but looking back I see Him working regardless.

During the time I spent in the military (1965-1968), the Vietnam War escalated from 50,000 troops to over 500,000. At the time I thought that I was just lucky to miss going over there to fight, but as I stated earlier luck had nothing to do with it. Combat troops were being deployed on a regular basis and 58,000 young men lost their lives over that ten year period.

After getting out of the Army I moved back home and got a job with ADT Alarm Company and married five months later.

My wife had been attending church for some time and is the one who guided me to start going to church and hearing the Word of God. I accepted the Lord in 1975.

Two things were always a desire of mine as far back as I can remember. Number one was Aviation and number two was Law Enforcement. I was fortunate to see both of these desires fulfilled. I was sworn in on October 17, 1969.

After 30 years in the Cleveland Police Department and raising four kids, my wife and I moved south to a small town in Georgia where my sister and her family had been living since the 1970's. We are currently active members in a Southern Baptist Church.

Looking back now I can see God was with me every step of the way whether I knew it or not. I'm at the point now where I can look back and see all that the Lord Almighty has done in my life. It humbles me so that there is no way I can possibly do enough to repay Him. The only thing I want to do now is to turn my life over to Him and let Him use me for His glory.

CHAPTER 1

THE POLICE ACADEMY
October 17, 1969 - January 15, 1970

Training

When I was first hired on the Cleveland Police Department, I had lived most of my life in the suburbs, except for the three years that I spent in the army. From childhood I had a bad inferiority complex. I was skinny and did poorly in school. The fact that I never bothered to study never entered my mind. At the age of 17 I got my driver's license and on it was my physical description. I was 5'7" and 125 pounds. So, as you can tell, I wasn't all that physically imposing in my early years. With my size, my poor self-image and my introverted nature I didn't socialize too much and had few good friends. However, I made great gains in all aspects during my tour in the army.

After getting out of the army I had no direction in life or any motivation to do anything about it. The only thing I ever remember wanting, other than flying, was to become a police officer. Every time a listing would be posted, I took the test, hoping to get on one of the police departments in the suburbs. There again, without preparing, I didn't do well. Each time my self-esteem hit a new low. However, that didn't stop me from applying for the next exam.

It was during the summer of 1969 the City of Cleveland was giving a test for the police department. At this time I had gotten married, had a son and was working for an alarm company, but I decided to try again. I figured, "What can I lose." Having served in the military gave me an automatic advantage of 10 points. I remember walking into the Convention Center where 1,000 other hopefuls were preparing to take the test. It was a general I.Q. test, nothing special. After taking the test, I felt I did fairly well but having failed before never expected it to go beyond that point.

I went back to living my life not thinking too much about it. Then after a couple of weeks I received a letter in the mail from the City of Cleveland informing me that I had scored 92% putting me 169 on the list. I can't tell you how thrilled I was with that score. I felt like this was the first time in my life my self-worth shot upward. I still had to take a series of tests including a lie detector, physical and physiological. I passed them all and entered the police academy on October 17, 1969. I couldn't have been happier in my life.

There were 200 of us that started the police academy, the first 100 on October 17 and the other 100 two weeks later on the 30th.

At the start we were attending classes eight hours a day five days a week. After a couple of weeks classes included Saturdays also. We received training in law, physical fitness, self-defense and firearms. At the end of each week we were required to pass a test in order to continue with the training.

At the end of the three months we had to turn in a note book containing the entire course which was worth a quarter of our score.

During training we were required to pass several shooting courses at the outdoor police range. The range consisted of several acres in a valley with high walls surrounding it. When we started going out there the sergeant in charge decided it would be a good opportunity to use us as cheap labor. It was the middle of winter and we were expected to work around the area cleaning it of debris. I had just gotten out of the army so I was used to taking orders and doing what I was told to do. After several weeks of going out there without shooting our weapons, we finally started to get training. One of the events that I found exciting was going around what was known as the rodeo. This was a required course where we would hang out the passenger window with a 12 gauge shot gun and drive on a round road course shooting at three steel targets. Later in my career I had to put this to practical use.

Autopsy

One of the requirements of the academy was to go to the county morgue to watch an autopsy. Fresh from the suburbs I was totally unprepared for a kind of life of being face to face with death on a regular basis.

About 30 of us arrived at the morgue mid-morning and gathered in a room that looked like something from the movies. The seats were in a semi-circle with the operating table in the middle. When we were all seated, the doctor came in. The first thing he said was he was worried he would not have a body to perform the autopsy but the Lord provided. He was a derelict found dead earlier that morning. He was probably in his late 50's but life on the street had aged him. The doctor explained everything he was doing and why. It was all very interesting and educational if you could get past the fact that this is a human body.

The process lasted a little over an hour with several in the class getting sick and leaving the room. I remember there wasn't the over powering smell that I would have associated with a morgue. I don't know what I was expecting but the examiner didn't hold anything back. He first cut a V-shape from the top of the victim's chest to the bottom of his stomach, then peeled the skin back to expose the muscles and bones. He then cut the rib cage apart with large cutters to expose the organs and removed each one for later examination to determine the cause of death. I got the impression he enjoyed demonstrating the procedure to a bunch of green young men. If I never see another autopsy again, it won't bother me one bit. It did prepare me, however for other things I would see while on the job.

The doctor who performed the examination, a seasoned coroner, had been around since the 1930's. During that time period 12 bodies were found in the city, some dismembered, several with their heads removed. The serial killings were later known as the 'Torso Murders'. Masks were made in hopes that the public might identify the victims. Several of the 'death masks' of these victims can be seen at The Cleveland Police Museum. Out of the 12 only three were eventually identified.

During the time Elliot Ness had come from Chicago to become the city's Safety Director. While Ness had little to do with the actual investigation, the murders were never solved and some say this was his downfall. In 1947 he ran for mayor and lost. Later in 1997 the son of Elliott Ness located his ashes in his attic and had a memorial service for him in which the entire police department took part.

CHAPTER 2

The Fourth District

1970 – 1973

In Cleveland, heavy coats were standard issue for the winter months. We referred to them as "horse blankets" because they were so big and heavy. After a while I got the idea that any time we were to go into a potentially dangerous situation, I would put my service revolver in the coat pocket and keep my hand on the gun. This way if there was any trouble I would be ready.

Another part of our uniforms were the service hats. You could always tell a rookie by his hat. Service hats had a wire band inside to hold their shape so they would always look good. The old timers would take the band out and pull the sides down to make their hats look well worn. In old WW II movies the pilot of the aircraft would often wear his radio headset over his hat to make the hat look used. This was called the 50 Mission Look. Knowing what the old timers were doing, the first thing we did as rookies was to remove the band.

We were required to put our hats on any time we would leave our patrol cars. Some supervisors would come down hard on you if they caught you without your hat on. I didn't understand what the big deal was nor did I like wearing the hat all of the time until it occurred to me that this was for our own safety. If there was a situation where there were a large crowd of people, or if the lighting was low and you could not make out who was who, you could always pick out an officer by his hat. Let's say for example you are searching a building when all of a sudden a shadow comes out of the dark. You can't tell who it is until you see the outline of the hat and you know it's your partner.

Learning the ropes

I graduated from the academy in January of 1970 and was assigned to the Fourth District. This was a time before desegregation. The City of Cleveland was divided into six Police Districts. The First and Second Districts located on the West-Side which were predominately white areas. The Third District was downtown and the Fourth, Fifth and Sixth Districts were on the Eastside, which was for the most part black. Everyone worth his salt wanted to work on the Eastside because that was where all of the action was. The Fifth District was considered the worst or best depending on your outlook.

The day before I was to report for duty I rode out to the area to check it out and get an idea of the location and where to report for duty. As I said in the beginning I'm from the suburbs. Here I was driving around the inner city not knowing a thing about the area. I passed the station house several times because I was expecting to see a big building that looked like a police station. What I finally found turned out to be a small brick building that had been built around the turn of the century and set back from the street.

I reported for duty with about four other rookies that had just graduated from the academy with me. We were each assigned to training officers who were to give us our real on-the-job training. I felt like a fish out of water. All of the preparation that I received from the police academy did nothing to make me ready for what police work, if you can call it that, was really like.

We were bounced around with different officers every day in order to get an all-around feel for the job. Boy was I in for a rude surprise.

As time went on, I started to become familiar with the area and the job and began to relax. As we drove around our assigned area, I was told to always know where I was by looking at the street signs so that if anything happened, I could tell someone our location.

It was several months into my new career, being bounced from different partners that I was becoming more and more disillusioned. With a few exceptions, my partners and supervisors were heavy drinkers. Back then I guess it was the normal thing to do because since they were in uniform they didn't have to pay for the drinks. I saw good men become alcoholics because of this. I also witnessed prisoners beaten unconscious or given broken bones. It was hard for me at times to see a difference between some of the officers and those being arrested.

I was young, naïve and wanting to fit in with the old timers; I went along with the program. Fortunately, I didn't get caught up in all the drinking. After a few months I was assigned to two regular partners who worked out great because now I didn't have to work with a lot of the hard core drinkers. They still drank a lot, but at least now we were doing police work, too. I was working three different shifts, rotating from 3rd to 2nd to 1st and they all started on the 1st of the month. Just as you began to get used to a shift, you would change. Let me tell you it was tough.

I was just hoping for a chance to be transferred out of the Fourth District to a specialized unit in the department.

It didn't much matter to me where; I just wanted out. At one point while in the Fourth District I had to fight not quitting because I had become so depressed. I didn't know what I thought or expected a police officer should be, but this wasn't it. It wasn't until 1974 that EMS and fire rescue started so part of our job was handling dead bodies and conveying people to the hospital. We were equipped with station wagons with stretchers. We were at the county morgue and all the area hospitals so much that we knew all the personnel by their first names.

The department back in the late 1960's was nothing like today. At that time the force was mostly white males. We had only one frequency on the radio for the entire city. You would rarely hear a black man and definitely no female voices on the air. The dispatchers at that time were, for the most part, retired officers. Having experience they knew how to give an assignment and who to give it to. That would all change in the 1970's. Unique with the times back then was that we had no portable hand held radios. If we were out of the car, the dispatcher would activate a frequency and our overhead lights would come on. That meant that if you were out of your car, you had better be able to see it. I remember times when some of the officers would park behind a bar and stay inside so long that when the dispatcher activated the lights, they were on so long they actually ran down the battery. When they got back into the car, it wouldn't start. How they got away with that I didn't know and I didn't want to know. I was just a rookie and I minded my own business.

I was becoming more and more disillusioned as time went on. On several occasions my partners were so drunk that they would pass out in the police car. I had one that stayed at the bar so long that when he got outside he leaned against the side of a building and threw up while in uniform and in public. Another time I ended up driving and handling all of the radio assignments myself while he slept in the back seat. One Saturday I was scheduled to drive the Lieutenant around for the tour of duty. We went from one bar to another and in each one he would have a shot and a beer.

We did this at a half a dozen places. Then he told me to drive and stay on the side streets. This was so no one could see him sleeping with his hat on and head hanging out the window. I'm not saying all the officers were drunks, but it sure seemed I got assigned to the ones that were.

As a young police officer I entered a totally unfamiliar environment. Here people behaved according to a culture of violence that I had never known. I recall one afternoon an off duty police officer, one of the old timers, was on his way to work in the Fourth District where he had worked his whole career. When at the intersection of East 131st Street and Harvard, he was struck broadside by a motorist who, traveling at a high rate of speed, crashed the red light. The officer was killed almost immediately on impact. While he lay there dying, the converging area youths decided to rob him of his gun, badge and anything else of value. Events such as this gradually change your outlook on life. People start to change little by little. Eventually it becomes you against them; the police against the citizens.

Another time while working the afternoon shift we responded to a fire in the neighborhood. The houses were old and run down. They were mostly made of wood. This particular night the winds were kicking up pretty good, gusting to about 40 M.P.H. So when one of the houses caught fire, the high winds carried the sparks to other homes catching them on fire, too. Before the night was over more than 35 homes burned to the ground. Admittedly that was a sight to behold all on its own but add to this picture people running in and out of their homes trying to rescue their belongings. They would bring items out of the house and place them on the front yard then go back in to get more stuff. When they came back out, all of their belongings were gone. They were being ripped off by their own neighbors.

Remember my mentioning the station wagons with the stretchers that we drove in order to handle all the emergencies in the city? I was assigned to drive a sergeant around for the night. We were working midnights and the only duty a street supervisor had was to check on his men, about four zone cars and make "calls" which is determining what kind of crime to call it for the reports. I was fairly new on the job and ready to fight crime. After a couple hours, the sergeant told me to drive to a park area and pull behind a back stop in the ballpark. When I did, he got out of the car, walked to the back, opened the back door and crawled into the back and lay down and went to sleep.

Now picture this! I'm 26 years old with maybe a year or two on the job and ready to go out there and clean up the streets. Here I sit behind the steering wheel while my sergeant is sleeping on the stretcher.

Shooting at East 116th Street and Buckeye

Looking back I realize how God has been working in my life even before I accepted His Free Gift of Salvation. One such incident happened January 2, 1972. We were working the 2nd shift and just happened to be having lunch at McDonalds with the officers working the A.I.U. (Accident Investigation Unit) car. It was late afternoon when my partner and I received a radio assignment to handle a damage accident at a nearby major intersection. Before we could respond one of the A.I.U. Officers volunteered to handle it for us. Thinking nothing else about it my partner and I went to another assignment of a domestic complaint. Around 18:15 we heard a frantic call over the radio of two police officers shot at the location of the damage accident we'd received earlier. By the time we got there, everything was over with. Come to find out the driver of one of the vehicles was intoxicated. He was in the back of the police car and when one of the officers informed him that he was going to be under arrest for D.U.I., he pulled out a gun and shot the officer in the head. The second officer was out of the car interviewing the other driver. After shooting the officer in the police car, he shot through the windshield striking the other officer in the arm. By this time other officers had arrived on the scene. The officer outside just opened up on the suspect striking him multiple times. When we got on the scene, the suspect was out of the back of the police car on the ground and was having muscle spasms, but was dead.

The officer that was shot in the head never fully recovered from his injuries. He retired from the force with a medical disability and passed away a few years later from complications due to the injuries. His personality changed and he was never the same. Prior to the shooting he was one of the best partners that I had worked with. He kept you entertained the entire shift by making everything humorous. He was upbeat all of the time. Afterwards he was withdrawn and very quiet. It broke my heart to see this once big strong man reduced to a shell of his former self. The third officer on the scene later became my partner for the next 13 years.

There is no doubt in my mind that God's hand was on me that night. Some people might say that it was just coincidence or just luck. But I know as sure as anything that it was a God thing. God Almighty directs the affairs of man and the path of a good man. I'm not saying that I'm a good man, but I'm redeemed by the blood of the lamb.

This was just a start of a journey that would take me to the very highs and lows of what this life can offer and looking back now I can see God was with me every step of the way whether I knew it or not.

Remembering Ernie

I had worked with the officer shot in the head prior to the shooting. He was the funniest man that I've ever known. I would laugh so hard that I couldn't stop. When interrogating a person about a petty crime, he would place him in the back seat of the zone car and explain that the overhead light would come on if the person lied. So here was this poor guy in the back of the police car intoxicated. When asked how many drinks he had, he stated, "Just two."

Immediately the light came on and he jumped and said, "Well maybe I had a couple more than two." Ernie would turn the light switch on and off to activate the light, but the suspect swore that it was a lie detector.

Another time we were called to a family fight in the ghetto. The couple was fighting with one another and had called the police. We got there and after a few minutes learned that this had been going on for years. Really there's nothing that we could do to solve the problem in just a couple of minutes. So Ernie suggested that if they were legally married and couldn't get along, the only solution was to get a divorce. They both were agreeable so Ernie said for both to place their right hands on his badge and he said, "By the power invested in me by the City of Cleveland I now pronounce you divorced." They were both happy about the situation and when we left they were getting along with each other just fine. Weird!

The inner city, which was the majority of our district, was predominately black so the culture was totally strange to me. A majority of the females were single mothers with multiple boyfriends. It wasn't unusual to have five or six kids all with different fathers. I'm not being racist or a bigot. I'm just stating what I have experienced in the inner city and I'm certainly not saying that that's the culture of the entire black community.

We would get a call of a female being beaten by a male in the street or at a residence. We would arrive on the scene and interview the female who was pretty beaten up. One of the first questions was, "Do you know who this male was that beat you up?" Most of the time the answer was that the woman didn't know who the man was other than that he was the father of her baby. When I first heard this statement, I thought that she was just putting me on. How can you have a baby with someone and not know who he is. I found this to be a common occurrence.

I also learned not to ask a possible suspect, "Where do you live?" You ask, "Where do you stay," because people with no steady jobs or income normally stay where ever they can. The usual answer was, "I stay at East 55th Street and Superior," or some other intersection. So the obvious question would be "so you live in the middle of the street under the street light?"

When we got a report of a possible suspect in a crime, we patrolled the area looking for the person matching the description. Often when we pulled over, got out of the car and tried to talk with this person, he started running. So here we go in a foot chase. When we finally capture this guy we ask him why he ran from us if he had nothing to hide. Nine times out of ten they would say, "Because you were chasing me."

Dead Baby

I remember one day I was working with one of my regular partners when we get a call of a sudden illness of a child at a house on Lower Buckeye Road. I was still fairly new and I still wasn't used to handling dead bodies. We responded to the scene with red lights and siren. We arrived within several minute of the call. We raced up stairs where we were met by the parents of the child. They escorted us into the back room where we saw a baby only a couple of months old laying in his crib. As new as I was on

17

the job I still recognized what is called lividity blood. That's where after death the blood pools at the lowest part of the body making it look like bruises. This occurred several hours after death so we knew immediately that he was dead. There were no signs of anything that would make us think that it wasn't just a natural death. No signs of injuries or violence. To save the parents from any more grief we picked up the baby and ran down the stairs and placed him in the police car and raced with lights and siren to the hospital as if he were still alive. I really don't know why we did that but at the time I guess we didn't want to tell them that their child was dead.

Motorcycle accident

Later on that same year I was working the 2nd shift (3 P.M. – 11 P.M.). I had just bought a new 350 Honda that I had been driving to work every day. I had been riding a motorcycle for a couple of years but this was the first one that I owned. It's about a 20 minute ride home from the station house. I had just left and started home. I had this routine down to a science. I would ride from East 131th. Street to East 93rd Street avoiding the traffic lights by adjusting my speed. From East 93rd Street to Broadway there were about three lights to miss. I had to have my speed to at least 55 to 60 M.P.H. to make it all the way to Broadway. I had gotten up to speed going down a hill. As I approached East 79th Street, I observed a car coming toward me in the opposite direction. As I passed the intersection I saw that this car was making a left turn into a bar. It all happened so fast that I really didn't have time to react. For a split second I thought that I had made it past him without getting hit. Well just as I was directly next to him, he turned striking the motorcycle on my left side knocking it out from under me which propelled me head first onto the roadway. From the momentum of going 60 M.P.H I slid face down on the street for about 75 feet ending up sliding to the curb. I normally didn't wear my face mask on my helmet, but for some reason I did that night. While sliding face first spread eagle, I saw sparks in front of my face as the face mask was ripped off the helmet. Without that mask my face would have been ripped off.

When I attempted to stand up, I found that my leg would not cooperate with me and I fell back down. A lady from a nearby house heard the accident and came over to help. Also to his credit the driver of the other vehicle came running down the street to check on my condition. My first thought was that I normally just stuck my revolver in the front of my pants on the way home.

You have to remember I was still young and dumb. So that was the first thing that I checked to see if it was still there. My heart sank finding it missing. I immediately identified myself as a police officer to the driver of the other vehicle and told him that my revolver was missing and asked him to find it.

A couple of minutes later he came back holding my gun. I stuck it into the front of my pants without checking on its condition. A few minutes later an unmarked detective's car arrived on the scene before anyone else. They helped me into the back of the car. When I got in, I pulled out my gun from the front of my pants to hand it to the detective for safe keeping. When I pulled it out, I noticed that the hammer of the revolver was cocked ready to fire. It would have taken less than a pound of pressure to pull the trigger discharging the gun. That was two bullets (tongue in cheek) I dodged that night.

We arrived at the hospital which was five minutes away and went directly to Emergency. I was quickly escorted into a private room. My clothes were torn to shreds and my boot that the car hit was torn half way off my foot. I had road rash on my knees and my arms had several layers of skin gone, but nothing was broken. The nurses had no mercy for me because they grabbed a couple of brushes and started to scrape my open sores with vigor cleaning them out. I almost flew off the table when they hit the open sores with those brushes. In the meantime my motorcycle was being transported home on the back of a tow truck. Needless to say it made it home that night before I did A friend of mine had called my wife to tell her that I "fell off of my motorcycle" which of course she couldn't figure out. The tow truck arrived at my house with this twisted hulk of what was once a motorcycle dangling from the back. When she saw that I guess she nearly fell through the floor. I wasn't there to witness the event. When I did get home, about a half hour later, I was pretty sore all over and looked like I had just come off the battle field with bandages all over my head, arms and leg.

Thinking back on what could have happened that night, again I saw it was a God thing. No doubt in my mind! (Funny how He never leaves a doubt about His presence in a given situation.) If I had turned a fraction of a second sooner, I would have struck the other vehicle broadside, sending me over the top at 60 M.P.H. The odds of my surviving that crash were not good. The gun I had stuck into the front of my pants could have easily gone off and shot me, and finally if I had not had the face mask on my helmet that day, which I generally never used, sliding down the street 75 feet face first I could only guess I wouldn't be so pretty today.

The Honda was pretty much totaled, but I lived by the theory that "if you get thrown off a horse, get right back on." I was off work for a couple of weeks recovering from my injuries, but as soon as I could move again I went out and bought a Harley Davidson Super Glide motorcycle. It was the biggest motorcycle around at the time. This one had to be kick started which means using your body weight pushing down on the starter level to get the engine started. I had one problem. My knees were still taped up from the accident and I couldn't use my weight to start the engine. Yea! I was pretty smart back then. I just figured, if you get thrown off a horse, get back on a bigger one. I had a lot of fun with that bike for a few years. Marital responsibilities and a third son made me decide my hobbies would have to be put on hold for a short time so I sold my Harley. It turned out to be 20 years. I was looking through a book of classic motorcycles at one time and kicked myself when I saw my red/white/blue Super Glide.

The realities of the Job

In my first three years on the department I handled probably over 100 bodies which included natural, accidental and homicides. Like I said I was just a young white boy that grew up in a white suburb never really exposed to this kind

21

of violence or this way of life. For example, one of the first homicides that I handled involved two brothers who were fighting over who was going to drive the car to church. The one shot and killed the other on the scene.

Another type of emergency we had to handle was births. A lot of officers had to deliver babies. Lower income citizens who had no hospitalization would wait to the very last minute before going to a hospital. Sometimes they waited too long. In those cases the baby wouldn't wait and the mothers would deliver them at home. Thankfully, I never had to deliver any babies, but I worked with a lot of officers that did and believe me from what they described there was no way that I wanted to go through that ordeal. It's something that's hard enough with your own wife, but having to deliver a baby alone was something that I could live without.

After dealing with such violence and witnessing what man can do to another man, you start to become callus to a whole slanted perspective of life. As a police officer you might handle 10 to 15 radio assignments a day. Each assignment is a negative situation, anything from a family fight, neighbor's fighting, dog barking, or who's going to drive the car to church. Over a period of time, day after day, week after week, year after year you become very negative about life in general. This profession has the highest suicide rate and the highest alcoholism rate second only to doctors. Oh, I almost forgot, and one of the highest divorce rates.

Mayor Ralph Perk

Early in the 1970's we had a mayor by the name of Ralph Perk. Now this man meant well, but had no clue how to run a large major city. It got to a point where the City of Cleveland became a national joke. The river that flowed through the city caught fire due to all the pollution that was being dumped into it. When the mayor was touring a steel plant, he was given a torch to attempt to weld a piece of iron and his hair caught on fire. His wife was just as strange. She was invited to the White House to dine with the first lady. She declined because that happened to be her bowling league night. Strange!

City finances got so bad that we would get our city checks every two weeks and ran to the bank to cash them before the money ran out. Some banks actually refused to cash them. The following is a letter to the editor that my wife wrote and the newspaper published to her surprise.

From the Cleveland Plain Dealer - December 1972
Police Are Defended:

Mayor Perk recently ordered 954 policemen to work eight to 20 hours overtime per week due to an increase in crime and a lawsuit from the NAACP. (This by the way was without pay.) "It is the police department's responsibility to drive crime off the streets," he said. This is to be done with a patrol car which is in the garage for repair the majority of the time and with an undermanned force.

The crime increase falls greatly upon Mayor Perk. He should look for legitimate explanations to the complaints and problems which arise instead of badgering the police department every time he gets a crimp in his neck.

These men gave up part of their constitutional rights, one of which being the right to speak out, to become a police officer. Now Mayor Perk wants to strip them of their manhood too. He allows them rags for uniforms and orders they be cleaned, pressed and well-groomed at all times, or they will go up on charges.

Mayor Perk, I'm sorry there is not enough thread left in the material to perform the requirements above. Soon there will be nothing but one big patch.

His unfair and unjustifiable accusations are helping to cause this crime increase. He is continually running these men into the dirt and therefore showing no respect towards them. How then can he expect the criminal, let alone the decent citizen, to respect the authority they hold when he lacks so much?

Mayor Perk's last order was put across as a form of punishment. He said if the police are not successful in reducing the crime rate at least 5% in December he will not allow them their clothing allowance and longevity pay which are long past due. He has already taken away the Christmas Day for which so many police have waited at least four years to spend together with families.

These are men with families and lives of their own. They are not little tin soldiers or puppets on a string to be kicked around and bounced back and forth whenever Mayor Perk gets a bug up his back.

Many such men have given up their lives to do their duty and all the police get in return is a slap in the face. If Mayor Perk would give them the respect they so highly deserve and think of them as men instead of a kicking post, the crime rate might decline more.

Mrs. Ruth Albright

Prisoner Transport

During this time in the districts one of the duties was to transport the prisoners that were arrested that day down to the central jail at the Justice Center commonly referred to as the J.C. This was done from all six districts in the early morning hours. Normally the O.I.C. of the district would call radio and assign one of the zone cars for transport. This was a fairly easy duty except if there were a large number of prisoners. Normally this required only two officers to transport up to 15 or 20 prisoners at a time. There was a prisoner van at each district for the haul. So we would return to the district to pick up the prisoners and the van.

After loading them up, we drove the 20 minutes downtown to the Justice Center. The J.C. housed all of the courts both county and city, all of the attorneys, the specialized units in the department, radio room, gym, chief of police, police academy and of course the city and county prison. The city side is a nine story building. Attached by walk ways is the 27 story county buildings. It's quite a large complex.

When we got to the J.C. we had to drive down a ramp to an overhead door that was manned by a county guard. The first door opened and we would drive in to another door. We would wait until the first door closed before we could drive into the garage. The way things were designed was that between the two doors were the elevators we used to take the prisoners up to the jail. Here comes the problem. Before we could go up in the elevator with all of the prisoners, we had to give up our guns to the guard on duty. Now remember that we were between two doors and we couldn't leave the van there so the driver would have to stay in the van, while the other officer transferred the entire group of prisoners up in the elevator alone and unarmed.

Normally this was no problem because most of the prisoners were in for intoxication or other minor violations, but I always worried that if someone got the bright idea to jump the officer in the elevator there was no one there to stop him. It's only a few seconds from the garage to the jail unit, but there could be a lot of damage done to an officer in that time. I always felt uncomfortable when I had to do the transport and thought that they could have come up with a better method.

Working the Night Shift

The night shift is a very depressing shift to work. For one thing you work all night and sleep during the day which is not natural. After two or three weeks you finally start to get acclimated to that shift and then must change to the 2nd shift. Back then we changed the 1st of every month rotating in reverse, from 3rd, to 2nd, to 1st. In the winter months when it gets dark at 4:00 in the afternoon, you barely get a glimpse of day light because you sleep until 2:00 or 3:00 in the afternoon.

On a normal night shift it's busy for the first few hours. After the bars all close down at 2:30 A.M. things start to settle down. Around 4 A.M. or 5 A.M. it's so quiet with nothing going on you start getting tired. So you would find a secluded place in your area, pull over and park to get a little sleep. I couldn't really sleep when we were parked. For some reason if I was riding and as long as the car was moving I would fall asleep, maybe because I felt secure.

This one night we found a parking lot with brick walls seven feet high on three sides. On the fourth side was the driveway. There was no other way in or out so we were pretty safe. Now normally I can't sleep if the car is not moving, but I was starting to relax and I decided to undo my gun belt so that I could really get comfortable by sliding down in the seat.

You get so accustomed to hearing your car number on the police radio that even half asleep when radio calls your number, you jump up and you're ready to go. As I was laying there I heard a broadcast of a male breaking into a business on Lee Road. He was seen running from the area. As they were giving the address number and the description of the suspect, I started to realize that the address they gave was the same address that we were sleeping behind. The next thing that I knew the suspect came running down the driveway towards our car. I got so excited that I jumped up from a crouched position and attempted to get out of the car to give chase forgetting that I locked the door and it wouldn't open. I finally got the door opened and jumped out of the car and started to chase the male. Then, I realized that I had taken my gun belt off and it was still on the front seat of the car. Talk about a bunch of Key Stone Cops. We were them. By the time I retrieved my gun and belt the suspect was long gone. Well after that I learned never to take the belt off while trying to sleep.

One day I reported for duty on the 3rd shift and attended roll call which was held at the front desk of the district. My regular partners were off that day so I was assigned to a new partner. Well you see how lax things were out in the Fourth District that the partner I was assigned to was actually carrying his pillow and an alarm clock. I knew right away I was in for a great time tonight. What was really bizarre was that no supervisor said a word to him about that.

A lot of the old timers loved working nights because they could sleep most of the night and be refreshed in the morning to go to their other job. This was a good deal for them. An interesting trick they devised was that all of the cars had a recall system as mentioned earlier. This was made up of both the overhead lights being activated and alarm like an alarm clock going off which was located under the hood. When it was time to go to sleep, he would get out of the car, go under the hood and disconnect the lights leaving the alarm on so when radio called the lights wouldn't work but the alarm would wake him up. Like I could have slept. What was wild was that after a while and when radio pushed the frequency which was two distinct tones you got to know yours just by the sound even before the lights came on.

While getting a good night's sleep we would get a radio assignment and then after a reasonable amount of time give it back depending on the assignment. It would be either a bad address, no response, or unable to locate. That way we didn't have to move. This was real nice. Like I had mentioned before during this time I was seriously considering quitting the job. I figured that if this was police work I didn't need it. Fortunately I stuck with it and things changed a great deal.

There were two other occasions that sleeping wasn't a good idea and one of them was almost fatal.

One night was just like any other night shift with nothing special happening. When I reported off duty, I went home and straight to bed. The next day when I arrived at work, I learned that one of the cars never reported off duty and no one knew where they were. They wouldn't answer radio broadcasts and their police car could not be located. A city wide search was started and cars from all over the city were called in, in an attempt to find the missing officers.

Finally police radio received a call from a construction company informing them that there was a police car in a school building that was still under construction and that the officers were not responding to an attempt to wake them. They were both rushed to the hospital where it was learned that apparently there was an exhaust leak. The fumes came into the car while they were both sleeping and they had been overcome. After several days in the hospital they were sent home. The one officer quit soon afterward because he ended up with a bad heart due to the incident.

Another time a zone car was parked on a main street in the middle of the night when no one was around. Both officers were apparently pretty tired because when they woke up it was broad day light and children on their way to school were passing this police car with two policemen sound asleep.

That wasn't the worst of their troubles. A newspaper reporter found out about it and took their picture. It appeared on the front page of the morning paper. Talk about having some explaining to do. They are probably still on the typewriter explaining what happened.

CHAPTER 3

IMPACT TASK FORCE – Free at Last!

1973 - 1975

Description of the Unit

In the early part of 1973 the City of Cleveland received federal money to start a program to fight violent crime in the city. This program was designed to work only the high crime areas during the time period when most violent crime occurred which was late evening to the early morning. The police department wanted young, eager officers that were ready to do the job as it should be done by putting the bad guys behind bars.

These men were recruited from all over the city from various departments including the districts, detective bureau, traffic and basic patrol. We were all mostly in our twenties with less than four or five years of police work. I had three years at the time. That means we were all chomping at the bit to get out there and do real police work. We were tired of being held back by "old timers."

We were divided into two shifts with four squads per shift. The three east side districts had the highest crime rate in the city. We even segregated ourselves from the rest of the department by moving to a city owned building so that we operated separate from everyone else. This made us feel pretty special.

Think about this scenario for a minute. Here you have 200 for all intent and purposes rookies told to go out there and clean up the crime. Wow! This was a little boy's dream. Make no mistake about it, in your twenties you are still a child at heart. The federally funded program was designed to cut down on crime in the city. It was an experiment of sorts to see if such a program could really work. We were given brand new cars, our own facility, our own radio frequency and dispatcher. We even had computers in our cars which in 1973 was unheard of. This concept was so far ahead of its time that it didn't take hold until the 1990's. We started to run checks on every car that remotely looked suspicious. We probably ran a hundred license plates a day with maybe one or two hits. We could run checks on weapons, stolen items and suspects. Our computers did cut down on waiting time through the radio dispatcher.

Another unique concept was that we would have just one partner and work with the same day off. I had been working with an officer from the Fourth District off and on for a couple of years. We both got on the Police Department two weeks apart and worked in the same area. So we both had about the same amount of experience. As it turned out, we would work together for another 13 years. We also lived in the same area in the western suburb of Cleveland so we rode to work together. I used to joke but it was true, I spent more time with him than with my own family. Working a good 50 hours a week together, we got to know each other so well that I would start a sentence and he would finish it, or vice versa. And I would just about get ready to say something and he would say it first. It got to be a little scary.

One great benefit was that whenever we got into a dangerous situation, we had no doubt about what the other one would do. This made for an ideal working relationship as it cut down on a lot of potential dangers of the job.

We would rotate from working day shift one month to the late shift the second month. There was no midnight shift which right there is a big plus. And we would rotate districts. Day shift in the Fourth District and then afternoon shift. The following month would be day shift in the Fifth District and then afternoon shift and so on working all three districts. We would be assigned only the priority one assignments which included robberies, homicides, felonious assaults and so on. We even got to wear our own patch that distinguished us from the other officers on the street. This was designed by a couple of our co-workers.

At the time that we started our unit there was another unit that had been in existence for quite a long time consisting of older officers with more experience. They were the Tactical Unit. These guys were called on to handle all dangerous situations that the district personnel couldn't. They were the prelude to the S.W.A.T. Unit. They had more enthusiasm than training. They would enter a drug house like gang busters arresting every one inside. When we came into existence, they were relegated to the other side of town which did not make them too happy. Here comes a bunch of rookies taking over their jobs. And of course the district personnel thought we were all prima donnas, so we weren't too loved anywhere we went. But we were having fun so we didn't worry too much about what others thought about us. We were finally doing police work the way we thought it was to be done. Scary!

During those two years as a unit we consistently made more arrests, gave out more traffic tickets, towed more cars and got into more accidents than the rest of the city combined.

In the early 1970's there were quite a few black militant groups stemming from the inner-city projects. These groups hated whites and hated white police officers even more. We were constantly being called into the neighborhood where they would set up an ambush. When the police car pulled up to the address they were shot at. Fortunately no one was injured most of the times.

Shooting Death of Fred Vacha

That soon changed on June 20, 1973, when one of our impact cars was working the second shift in the Fourth District. The following is the account of what happened by the surviving officer. This all started around 1:15 A.M.

Patrolman Saccany said he and Officer Vacha were on routine patrol when they spotted a man acting suspiciously near the bus stop at East 89th Street and Buckeye. They thought he might be a potential mugger. The officers drove around the block and returned for a closer look. Saccany stopped the patrol car. Vacha started to get out. "I'd like to talk to you for a minute," Vacha said to the man. With that, the man pulled a gun from his pocket and sprayed the car with gunfire. Three shots struck the hood, another hit a fender and one pierced the windshield. One shot struck

Vacha in the head. Another shot hit Saccany. Saccany said he jumped out of the cruiser and emptied his gun at the suspect. The man ran north on Buckeye, jumped a fence and disappeared. Scaccany radioed for help. Thirty patrol cars converged on the area and a massive search began.

Officer Saccany was 29 years old and Officer Vacha was only 25 years old. He died a short time later in the hospital. My partner and I along with a couple dozen other officers started a door to door search. We searched the area until sun up when one of the Tactical Unit team located the suspect hiding in the weeds about 100 feet from the shooting. The only reason that he did not escape was because of the quick response time of the other officers converging on the area. After checking the weapon, it was discovered that it had jammed and the only reason the suspect couldn't clear the weapon was because of all of the police officers around all night long.

In the notes I jotted down shortly after the shooting, I stated, "During the search my partner and I were standing not more than 10 feet from the suspect. We were standing there for about five minutes trying to figure out which way that he might have gone. When he was found lying in the grass he still had the gun with him and within arm's reach, not more that 2 or 3 feet away."

Come to find out that Fred Vacha was working his day off covering for another officer. He should have been off that day. Sometimes officers would with the approval of the supervisor change days off for different reasons. From what we learned later, they were coming up behind the suspect who was wearing a Muslim robe that covered most of his body. As the officers approached this male, at about 10 feet to 20 feet away, he pulled out a gun and without any warning started shooting. The first bullet went through the windshield striking Officer Vacha in the head which probably killed him instantly. The next shot hit the hood of the vehicle penetrating the firewall striking Officer Saccany in the heel of his foot. Apparently this male belonged to a Muslim group and was waging a holy war against America. As always the police officer on the street is the first target for any whacko that has a problem with the government. This was just the start of a deadly period in the unit that had so much promise in the beginning.

Stein and Kunchick

Tragedy struck again a short time later for two members of our unit. Only this time it took two other people with them. We learned about the accident the next day when we reported for work. It is hard to deal with the loss of two people you just saw the day before. What we learned later and from the newspaper account was they were driving home from a party around 4:00 A.M. Kunchick was driving along with his wife Mary Ann. In the back of the car were Bob Stein and a girlfriend, a Miss Alice Petrich. According to the police, they were traveling at a very high rate of speed on the interstate and as they approached a curve, the car went into a skid. It slid sideways into a parked steel hauler on the side of the road. The impact of the crash almost squeezed the two sides of the car together. According to the Brooklyn Police, several overhead lights that lit the curve where the accident occurred were out. They also said excessive speed and the wet pavement

36

contributed to the accident. This was just two more deaths in the newly formed Impact Task Force, but unfortunately they would not be the last.

Shooting Death of Bill Shapiro

About a year later there was another officer-involved shooting. This time one of the members of the Tactical Unit was involved. We were working out of the same city owned building so we got to know each other pretty well. On this particular day they were getting ready to go out on a drug raid. In fact we were joking around with him and his partner as they were leaving the building.

My partner and I were working the Sixth District when we heard over the Tactical radio that there was a shooting in the Fourth District and that there was an officer shot. We screamed through traffic getting to the area in record time.

When we arrived on the scene, it was chaos. They had the traffic stopped and were searching every car in line. With about 50 officers we started a search of the area which was mostly open field. We learned that after the raid, the Tactical Unit was rerouted back to the office when they responded to shots being fired in the area of Fairhill Road which happened to be a very steep hill with a high cliff on one side and a steep drop off on the other side. The suspect was on top of the cliff shooting down at the cars as they were driving up. The Tactical Officers approached the suspect from behind. As they got near him, he spun around shooting at Officer Shapiro striking him in the throat just above his bullet proof vest. After the shooting the suspect jumped down the cliff and made his escape down the other

37

side disappearing into the woods. They rushed Bill to the hospital which was only a couple of minutes away, but he was dead on arrival due to the loss of blood.

We along with most of the department searched for the suspect the rest of the day until dark. The supervisor called us off the search and had us return to the office. When we got back, we learned that the suspect had been found hiding in a drain pipe. We were all exhausted by now but happy that the suspect had been caught.

Cleveland Plain Dealer Article

December 1976

Cleveland Police last night arrested a 21 year old man in the back yard of a Cleveland Heights home and held him for questioning in the shooting death yesterday of Cleveland Tactical Unit patrolman William N. Shapiro.

The capture came about seven hours after Shapiro was blasted in the neck with a 12-gauge shotgun at Fairhill and Baldwin.

Shapiro was shot at point-blank range about 1:50 P.M. after he and three other Tactical Unit policemen went to the reservoir area to investigate reports that a sniper was shooting at cars on an embankment 100 feet above the road.

Shapiro, his partner William Sallupo and two other Tactical Unit patrolmen were sent to the Fairhill-Baldwin area after police received reports that a sniper was shooting at cars from the top of the embankment. The gunman apparently had left by the time they got there. But they waited and the man returned. Shapiro and Sallupo chased him, but lost him after a short distance. The four policemen spread out and were poking through the underbrush when Shapiro was shot.

The suspect was captured about seven hours later hiding beside a garage around 8:44 P.M. The hunt for Shapiro's killer at one time included more than 200 policemen and FBI agents, two airplanes, two helicopters and three police dogs.

The homicide unit day shift was held over while the search continued. Afternoon shift homicide unit detectives reported for work early. Off-duty members of the unit reported in voluntarily to take part.

That's four officers that we knew and worked with gone in less than a year and a half. We had hoped this would be the end to all these unnecessary deaths but unfortunately it wasn't. During the two years that the unit was in existence, we lost a total of five officers who were all from the same squad. After the shooting death of Officer Vacha and the off duty deaths of Officers Kunchick and Stein, we lost another one in a motorcycle accident. He was going home through the Metro-park when he lost control and hit a tree. They took him to the hospital and apparently there were no outward signs of injuries so he lay on a stretcher for what we heard was quite a long time. No one was aware that he had internal injuries, and he eventually bled to death waiting to be looked at. Another wasted life. A short while later another officer died of a rare blood disease. Including Officer Shapiro we lost six good men in two years. These were healthy, young men just starting off in life. It was unheard of losing so many in such a short time due to various causes.

You become very cold about life after seeing so much death and destruction. I can only compare it to being in a war zone eight hours a day. I remember a few times on my way home from work after putting in a particularly hard night handling say a triple homicide and cleaning up afterwards, I would think that these suburbanites going to work in the morning had no clue about the real world. They were leaving there homes in suburbia, driving to their jobs, parking in a guarded parking lot, going to their air-conditioned offices and then returning home that night. They would turn on the television watch the news about all of the crime and say, "What a shame," and then go to bed and start all over again the next day.

Chase with Shots Fired

After completing roll call on the 2nd shift, we were getting ready to get on the road and call in service. We were still at our lockers in the Amstan Building when we heard over the radio that a traffic car was chasing a suspect wanted in a bank robbery. There were probably a half a dozen cars with their crews ready to hit the streets and when we heard the chase we all got into our cars and attempted to join in. Of course this is what we live for: good chase, or shoot out, or a riot or anything else to get the adrenaline flowing.

We hit the streets running and joined the chase which was in the area of our office so we were there in no time. We were going up and down the side streets and were doing in excess of 80 M.P.H... The guy we were chasing headed north on East 26th Street which was a dead end at the railroad tracks. We were about the third or fourth car in the caravan. As we came to a crest of a hill, I noticed something flying out to the suspect's car on the passenger's side. As we approached what looked like a pile of clothes, there was something about it that I thought didn't look right. I yelled to my partner to stop the car so that I could go back and check on what was in the street. As we came to a stop, I got out of the car and heard shots coming from the area where the suspect's car was. Not knowing where the bullets were going I just got low and ran up the hill away from the shooting to check on what was in the street. As I approached the pile, I recognized it as the body of a female. As I said we were the third or fourth car in the chase, and I saw at least two of the other police cars run over the girl after she jumped from the fleeing car. There was total confusion at this time because there were so many police cars on the scene and so much activity. It was hard to figure out what was going on.

We called E.M.S. to take the girl to the hospital, but from the looks of her I didn't think she would make it. She had to have multiple broken bones and internal injuries after jumping from a speeding car and being run over by several more cars.

We then ran down the hill to check on what all of the shooting was about. As we got down there, we noticed that one of the suspects had been shot and was lying on the ground. A second suspect, his girlfriend, was in custody. Instead of waiting for a second ambulance we decided to take the wounded suspect to the hospital in the police car.

We put him in the back of our car and raced to the nearest hospital.

After a while the doctor came back and told us that the suspect was going to recover. The bullet had passed through the upper right part of the chest. We also found out that the female that jumped from the car was the mentally retarded sister of the suspect's girlfriend. She got scared during the chase and jumped out. She would recover but would be a cripple the rest of her life.

Now here comes the interesting part of the story. There were actually two chases going on simultaneously. One was just for a traffic violation and the other was the bank robbery. We thought we were chasing bank robbers. In fact we were chasing the traffic violator. The traffic car couldn't believe that one of our cars would actually shoot a motorist for breaking a traffic law. We don't know what happened in the real felony chase other than the suspect had gotten away.

We learned later that this poor guy was just up from West Virginia looking for work in the big city and had his girlfriend and her sister with him. He didn't have a driver's license so when the traffic car attempted to pull him over, he ran. I can imagine what this guy thought, "Here I come to the big city and the police shoot me for driving without a driver's license. Hate to see what would have happened if I was involved in a more serious crime."

Stripped Auto

One night when we were working the 3rd shift (11:00-07:00), my partner and I were in the lower part of the Fifth

District. It was around 3 A.M. and we were just cruising up and down side streets not really doing much of anything. It was a slow night during the week. When you aren't doing anything you normally drive very slowly about 10 to 15 M.P.H. just looking around for anything unusual. Talk about unusual because what happened next we weren't expecting. Sometimes when you are working the street things go from tragic to downright funny. This was so bizarre I couldn't believe what I was seeing. As we pulled to a stop at a stop sign, we noticed a car driving by pushing another one. Well normally this isn't too unusual, except the car being pushed was totally stripped. It was nothing but a frame, no seats, no fenders, no hood, no trunk, just the frame with tires used to get rid of the car sitting on a wooden box. Steering the car was this little old man. We both just sat there as the cars passed us not believing what we were seeing. When the second car spotted us, he high tailed it out of there leaving the old man to face the music alone.

We didn't give chase to the push car because we figured why chase it when we have the one without an engine or anything else for that matter. We pulled up to the stripped out vehicle and grabbed the old man. We started to question him about who the other guy was and what he was doing. Well he told us a story that we could not help but believe. He said that the other guy was his nephew and that he paid him $20.00 to steer the car to the drop off spot. Now how can you not believe a story like that? While working the streets you never know what is around the next corner and I mean it literally.

Fairhill Fatality

I was working the Accident Investigation car in the Fifth District. At that period of time each district had their own AIU car. Now, of course, they work out of a central location at the Justice Center. This was my first time working this car, and I wasn't really trained to handle serious or fatal accidents. These were handled by specially trained officers that go to school to learn the intricacies of investigation such as drawing a sketch of the scene to scale, making measurements on the scene and making note of the weather. This is just the beginning of the investigation. There are a number of reports to complete, so when we got our first fatal of the night I was grateful that I was working with an experienced officer.

I was filling in for the regular AIU officer who was off that day. We were working the afternoon shift when around 6:00 P.M. we got a call of an accident at East 127th Street and Fairhill Road.

We responded to the scene. Upon arrival we saw that a car going at a high rate of speed had hit the medium which was raised a foot above the roadway. When the driver hit the median, his car went airborne and landed on top of an oncoming car which flattened the roof crushing the driver instantly. When he landed on the oncoming car, the impact broke the left front wheel but his car was still able to be driven. Apparently, the driver panicked and fled the scene, but as he drove away, the broken wheel left a dark skid mark on the road. We couldn't believe that someone could be dumb enough to think we would not be able to follow the marks and locate the car. Which is exactly what we did. Not only did he try to escape the area, but he actually drove to his house. We followed him south on East 127th Street to Woodland, up to East 130th Street across Shaker Boulevard and Buckeye to South Moreland until we came to Forest Avenue where he turned west.

Half way down Forest Avenue he turned into a driveway where we found the car parked. From there on it really didn't take a seasoned investigator to figure out who the car belonged to and who was driving it. The driver was placed under arrest and booked in connection with Aggravated Vehicular Homicide. I just love it when we are dealing with criminal geniuses. Contrary to what is depicted on TV, real life criminals are mostly opportunists. When they see a victim, they go for it without much thought.

Such was the case when my partner and I got a call to a deli that had just been robbed in the Fifth District. This is pretty much a routine call that we got all of the time. So we didn't think too much about it. When we arrived on the scene, we asked for a description of the suspects so that we could get the information out on the air to the other cars. The next question was routine, but the answer was something that I didn't expect. When I asked for the description of the car that the thieves were driving the store clerk pointed outside and said, "That's their car there, parked in front of the store." Apparently the suspects got so excited that when they robbed the store they set their car keys on the counter, and in their haste to get away, they forgot the keys. When they attempted to drive away, they couldn't find their keys so they had to leave the car where it was and flee on foot. Geniuses!

East 55th Street and Superior

My partner and I were on routine patrol in the Fifth District one summer night. It was fairly quiet which was unusual considering the area and time. We were driving up Superior at about East 55th Street when we heard over the radio that a Fifth District zone car was chasing a stolen car, and that they were heading north on East 55th Street coming our way. We decided to pull over and wait for the chase to pass us so we could join in. We stopped on Superior on the northeast corner facing west. It wasn't more than a couple of minutes we could see the cars approaching. My partner was driving at the time which was unusual because he normally rode and handled all of the reports while I would do the driving.

As the cars approached, we were ready to pull out and join in on the chase. Just as the stolen car got to the intersection, the driver decided to attempt a right hand turn. The main problem with this decision was that he was still traveling well over 70 M.P.H. which makes it kind of difficult at that speed. It didn't take a genius to figure out what was going to happen next. When we realized that he was going to try and make the turn, my partner attempted to pull out of his path. But due to his speed and lack of reaction time we were struck on the left rear of the patrol car. The impact was so great that we were thrown into the intersection spinning us 180 degrees and knocking our overhead lights off the car throwing it another 75 feet across the street. When everything stopped moving, we jumped out. I pulled my gun and pointed at the driver screaming for him to get out. You have to remember that my partner and I were almost killed due to some low life that decided to run from the police, so my emotions were at an all-time high. Later I realized that I had my gun cocked and at that point it would have only taken a small amount of pressure to pull the trigger. I was very fortunate that the gun didn't accidentally discharge.

Later as we sat down to review the incident and make reports, we realized that if it hadn't been for that split second that my partner attempted to get out of the way, the suspect would have hit us broadside instead of the left rear over the rear axle. Hitting us there probably saved our lives because the axel took the full impact of the crash. Again, one could say we were lucky!

Chase to Willoughby

One afternoon my partner and I were in the Sixth District working the afternoon shift. We were always on the lookout for stolen cars and any suspicious activity in the area.

As we were riding up St. Clair Avenue around Five Points, we observed this car being driven by what looked like a juvenile. There were three other juveniles in the auto with him. We got behind him and ran a check on the vehicle through radio. A short time later radio came back and said that the car was just now being reported stolen. We attempted to stop them by turning on our overhead lights and hitting the siren. Guest what? They decided not to stop. So here we go! This idiot not only failed to stop but was driving past his friends waving to them like he was in a parade. He was driving at normal speeds at this point. Well here we go up and down side streets doing this parade thing. In the meantime my adrenalin was starting to flow and I was losing it. This guy started to get to me because of his total disregard of our attempt to stop him. Eventually we made it to the freeway where he entered going eastbound accelerating up to speeds of over 100 M.P.H.

When I went through the academy, one of the courses that we had to pass was something called the rodeo. In the rodeo an officer would ride in the front passenger side of the car and hang out the window so that the top half of his body was outside of the car while holding the shot gun. There were three steel targets to hit as the car went around in a circle.

My partner was driving this day, and we were broadcasting our location as we went so as we entered a suburb the local police department could be aware of what was going on and assist in the pursuit. At one point in the chase my partner attempted to pull alongside the vehicle while doing well over 100 M.P.H. As we got alongside, the suspect attempted to ram us; and at this speed it wouldn't have been a pretty sight after the crash. Now I really wanted to stop this guy before he hurt himself or someone else like my partner or me.

As we approached one of the eastern suburbs, I could see up ahead that there were a lot of flashing lights that looked like a road block. The suspect was not slowing down which wasn't a good thing. As we passed the police cars, a dozen officers holding shot guns and pistols got out of their cars and started shooting at the car as it went by. The problem was we were not more than a car length away from the suspects and were traveling at an excessive speed! We could have easily been hit, too. When I saw all the shots being fired, I instinctively ducked my head hoping not to get shot by the good guys.

We were going so fast at this point that no other police cars could possibly catch up. It was up to us to stop this maniac. This was the first time that I tried to use the rodeo technique of hanging out the window shooting at a moving vehicle. At this speed there was no way I was going to hang out the window like we were taught. Instead I just stuck the barrel of the shot gun out taking aim not to hit anyone in the car. The problem with this was I'm left handed and from the passenger's side I was going to have to shoot right handed. I aimed low hoping to hit the gas tank, not to blow it up but to disable the car.

We were so far from the city now that we had lost communications with our radio dispatcher and were unable to tell anyone of our location. As we approached an exit, the suspect pulled a quick move exiting at the last minute. We passed the exit so we turned and went up the entrance ramp. As the suspect fled north, he was losing control of the vehicle. Apparently I had shot out both left-side tires. After a couple of miles he made a quick right turn onto a small road. As he turned, he lost complete control ending up on someone's front lawn almost hitting his porch.

I was so hyped up at this point that all I wanted to do was drag this kid out of the car and beat him senseless. Fortunately I just pulled him out not too gently and placed the cuffs on him while my partner took care of the others in the car. Within just a couple of minutes 20 police cars from every suburb that we passed through arrived. It looked like a police convention.

After booking the suspects and towing the car back to the Sixth District, we started our paper work. The police department ran on paper work. When the car got to the garage, we went out to take a look. I was stunned to see how much damage I caused with the shot gun. The department used double o buck which is equal to 8- 32 cal. shots. The rocker panel was ripped off. Both left side tires were flattened. There were grooves along the side and trunk areas. It was a mess. As it turned out the suspect was the son of an employee of the car owner. The owner decided not to press charges. However, the kid was charged with multiple traffic citations and with an attempted felonious assault on a police officer as he'd attempted to run us off the road.

CHAPTER 4

Tactical Unit
1975 - 1976

After the break-up of the Impact Task Force Unit and the old Tactical Unit, we were all sent out to various districts. We were now known as the Tactical zone car. There was one car per shift in each district. At this point in time, we really had no formal training in tactical situations. We just had a lot of enthusiasm. We had the special equipment in the trunk of the car and in case of a situation such as a hostage taking, all of the cars from all over the city would respond.

Shots fired at East 66th Street and Chester

We were working the second shift, and after several hours into the shift, we got a call of a male shooting from a second floor apartment window. The lieutenant on the scene requested the Tactical car respond. We got the location and started heading that way. The location was one block north of Chester Avenue off of East 66th Street. We were headed west on Chester and as we approached the scene, we noticed that there was an open area between us and the suspect's apartment on Lucerne, a short street running from East 66th Street to East 69th Street.

As I came to a stop, I could see the suspect's apartment. All of a sudden there were shots being fired, and I could see small puffs of dirt flying up next to the car not more than five feet away. The old saying is, "That if you can see the house, the house can see you." I put the car in reverse and floored it to get out of the line of fire. Once behind cover, we got out of the car and started to get the equipment that we needed for the situation. We made our way toward the apartment and took cover behind some trees. I could see the lieutenant standing under the suspect's window pointing up identifying the location of the suspect. There was another car on the scene but when we arrived, they gave the problem to us to handle. We had the 37 mm teargas gun with several canisters. The shell is about 12 inches long and about 2½ inches wide and fits into a long barrel rifle. You break it down like a shot gun and then drop the projectile into it, close it up and you're ready to shoot. As we readied ourselves, the suspect continued shooting at us. The lieutenant was still standing in the open under the suspect's window, pointing upward at the suspect.

I took aim and fired. My shot hit the top part of the window frame causing the canister to ricochet back over the heads of the officers. This created a problem because none of us were wearing gas masks. I aimed and shot again. This time the ricochet went straight down and the lieutenant was gassed. Now I was starting to look bad. I adjusted my aim toward the bottom of the window which did the trick. The shot went right into the apartment. I put several more canisters into the apartment. After a few minutes the officers made it inside. The suspect refused to give up and fought with them. Finally he was subdued.

After more training on the weapon I found that the projectile would rise as it flew through the air instead of dropping like I thought it would. From then on I had no other problems which was fortunate because I had many occasions to use it.

Later on in my career, while in S.W.A.T., we responded to a call of an armed suspect held up in a house on the east side of the city. Upon arrival I was ordered, as the sniper, to find a secluded location where I had a view of the house and still had cover. In this area of the city the homes were close together with only a driveway separating them. I positioned myself in a fairly secluded spot on top of the garage in the rear of the house. The garage was constructed in such a way that the roof slanted downward and away from the dwelling making it the ideal location.

After several hours of negotiating with negative results, it was decided to make entry into the house. The plan was for me to deploy teargas into the rear bedrooms and drive the suspect to the front of the house. Up until now we had no idea where the suspect was. Once I deployed the teargas the entry team was to wait a few minutes and then enter, hoping the teargas had forced the male where we wanted. This was a small inner city home with three small bedrooms, a living room and a kitchen. The entry team was situated on the side of the house in the driveway awaiting my shot. I was only about 30 feet away so there was no problem hitting the window. I took aim at the rear window at a slight angle. When I shot, the projectile went through the rear window and out the side window next to the team.

What I didn't see from my viewpoint was a second window in the bedroom. Fortunately the entry team already had their gasmasks on.

Arrest of 32 Hells Angels

We had an occasion to make an arrest of 32 members of the Hells Angels Motorcycle gang.

Newspaper article was as follows:
Cleveland Press, December 1976

Thirty-two Hells Angels Motorcyclists were arrested in a St. Clair Ave bar early today in connection with the abduction and gang rape of a 21 year old woman on the East Side last week.

Police Tactical Unit members rounded up the 32 without resistance or violence at Bill's Traven, 5301 St. Clair Ave.

It was believed that among those arrested were four Hells Angels indicted by the County Grand Jury yesterday in connection with the abduction-rape.

Other indictments were expected to be returned, presumably against some of those arrested this morning.

The woman, a member of the Women's Army Corps home on leave from Fort Belvoir, Va., was walking her dog on Euclid Ave. east of University Circle at noon Thursday when she said five men forced her and the dog into a car with them.

She told police she was forced to commit a sex act in the car and then was taken to an East Side address where she was repeatedly raped by 14 men.

At about 10 o'clock that night, she said she was allowed to take her dog outside and flagged a passing motorist.

He dropped her off at University Hospitals but she went to the home of a friend, she said. The friend talked her into going to St. John Hospital for treatment. She had suffered face and chest bruises.

Police said the gang tattooed her right wrist with a star and half-moon. The woman also reported the gang took her purse containing $105 and silver necklace.

One of the suspects that was arrested served 10 months in the workhouse after pleading guilty to manslaughter in connection with the brawl in 1971 at Polish Women's Hall, 7526 Broadway, in which one Hell's Angel and four Breed cycle gang members were slain.

When we were called in for the briefing, we were told to expect trouble because this was a violent motorcycle gang known for their violent criminal activities. There were about 30 of us and we were prepared for anything that might happen.

We arrived on the scene in the early morning hours and pulled up in a caravan. We all jumped out and ran into the bar not giving them a chance to react. We circled the room so that no one could escape or react to our raid of their domain. They were told by the sergeant what was going to take place. We took them one by one out to the waiting prisoner van after searching them then conveyed them all downtown to the jail unit.

When we got to the jail they were told to take everything out of their pockets and place the contents on the counter. Let me tell you I have never seen anything like it. They were pulling pins, buckles, metals and all other items that could be used as weapons. By the time we were finished booking them there were so many homemade weapons that we would need a truck to haul it away. It was around 7:00 A.M. when we finally made it home. The following Saturday morning around 11:00, our sergeant was up in our office on the second floor of the Justice Center doing paper work when all of a sudden six Hells Angels walked in unannounced. You can imagine the shock and surprise that he felt when he looked up and saw these bikers in their colors. One of the members had his vest (which is the most important thing that they own) taken from him the night of the raid and wanted it back. Well there was no need to keep it so it was returned to him.

When they left, the sergeant got on the phone and chewed out the security guard down at the front door for not calling ahead of time and warning him that they were on their way up. This was before the metal detectors so they all could have been carrying weapons, and if they wanted to do harm to the sergeant they very well could have.

CHAPTER 5

FIFTH DISTRICT TACTICAL CAR
1976 – 1978

North Royalton Test

In 1976 after the Impact Task Force and the Tactical Unit were disbanded, I was in the Fifth District working a zone car. After working the same area and dealing with the same old assignment only with different players, I started to become depressed. I could see no future other than working a zone car in the ghetto my whole career. I was living in the suburbs about 25 miles from work and would have to drive 50 miles daily.

I heard that my local police department needed officers and was testing. I figured this would be a great opportunity for me to get away from the inner-city and work in a predominantly affluent white suburb where I would only be a couple of minutes from home. So I went for it.

There was the written test first and if you passed, you were required to take a physical and a psychological test. After passing all you were placed on an eligibility list.

I took the written test, and after a few weeks I got my score back. I placed number four out of a couple hundred. So I figured that with that score and my experience working in a large city police department my chances of being hired were really good. Also taking the test was the deputy chief's son who placed 70. The deputy chief was also a member of my home church. They were planning on hiring only seven people, so there was no way that his son could be hired with a score like that. Little did I realize the power of politics.

When I went for the psychological test, I found that it would be an all-day affair. There were probably 40 different tests taking about 8 hours with an hour for lunch which I passed on because I just wanted to finish. I passed the physical test that was given on a Saturday without any problem. Well I waited and waited without hearing back from anyone. After several months one day after church the chief came up to me and told me that I wasn't going to be hired because according to the results of the psychological test it was determined that I would not be happy in the suburbs after working in a major city, and that I would probably quit after a short period of time. This was a stunning blow to my ego. I couldn't believe that they would reject me because of something that might or might not happen. Needless to say I was depressed and discouraged, but little did I know that what the Lord said about the 'path of a righteous man' was in play here.

After a while I kind of got over being rejected and didn't think too much about it until I found out that the chief's son had made it. Then things started to fit together. How could someone that was 70th on the list get hired when they were hiring only seven people? Now I'm not saying that there were any politics involved but it sure seems funny about the outcome. They had to pass over about 60 people to get to the chief's son.

As I look back on this, I realize that I probably wouldn't be happy working in a small suburban community where everyone knew your business and where real police work wasn't done too often. The department was basically there to make the citizen feel like they were being protected by competent officers which was just an illusion. Now that I am retired and can reflect on my career, I realize that it would have been a big mistake to take that job because I would have missed out on all of the good experiences and opportunities of being in a large city police department. The thing that I hated about it turned out to be the best part. I would have missed being a S.W.A.T. officer for nine years and then a sergeant for the last 12 years on the force. I also would have missed being able to fly and get paid to do something that was my passion for eight years and then of course being in the motorcycle unit for the last two years. Not only was I in the motorcycle unit, but I was the Officer-in- Charge. That was the unit that I wanted to be in from the start of my police career. Now tell me that God Almighty isn't in charge of things and knows what's best even if we don't agree at the time. He loves his children even if they are unlovable, disrespectful and disobedient.

Terminal Tower

August 26, 1976, we reported for duty at the Justice Center. Around 10:00 A.M. we got a call from police radio that there was a hostage situation with shots fired at the Terminal Tower Building. We all gathered for a briefing. We got our orders and equipment, loaded up our vehicles and headed to the area.

When we got to the building, we learned that there was a lone gunman on the 36th floor holding 10 hostages.

Newspaper Article Following:
The Cleveland Press Aug. 26, 1976

Seven held by gunman in Terminal Tower. A man, armed with two guns invaded the 36th floor offices of the Chessie executives shortly after 10 AM, fired two shots to announce his presence and demanded full GI veterans' benefits for all Chessie employees.

The gunman was identified as Ashby Leach, 30 of Huntington W. Va., a Vietnam War veteran. High-ranking police and FBI agents crowded the 36th floor outside the main door to the Chessie headquarters, trying their best to maintain communications with Leach. They reported the hostages were in good condition.

At first Leach held 10 persons but he allowed two women to go free, using them to carry messages to police while he held guns on them. According to police, Leach entered the reception office of President Watkins, at 10:10 AM, armed with a sawed off shotgun and a handgun. He fired two shots into the ceiling. He kept saying he had been deprived of his GI Bill Rights when he formerly worked for Chessie. He forced Robert McGowan, administrative vice president and one of the hostages, to type out his list of demands for Chessie employees to get full benefits.

He walked Vivian Cousino, a secretary to the door and handed the list to the police outside. He re-reentered the reception room. She stayed outside. He ordered police to send her back in. We can't. She collapsed. We've taken her to a hospital," he was told. It was not true but he didn't protest.

Some of the 36th floor personnel made their escape by private elevator when they heard of the gunman holding hostages.

FBI agents joined the tactical police force and plainclothesmen who rushed to the Terminal Tower. One of the FBI men was Bernie Thompson, an expert in negotiation for hostages, the man who talked bank robber Eddie Watkins into giving up after holding hostages in a West Side bank overnight.

When the gunman made his presence known, a Chessie employee managed to alert Jerry Burrows, Terminal Tower superintendent. He called police and ordered the evacuation from the floors Chessie occupied. Police quickly sealed off those floors and cleared Public Square's walks of pedestrians in front and back of the tower. Traffic was blocked on Prospect behind the Terminal Tower complex.

Leach was reported to be in his 20's. According to Milton Dollinger, assistant vice president in charge of public affairs, he worked as an apprentice for Chessie in Huntington three years age, then was laid off. Dollinger said he again applied for a job three months ago but was not rehired. "We don't know how he got here or how he explains his grievance."

Police ordered removal of the revolving door at the tower's main entrance as a precautionary measure in case stretchers had to be used. They set up their command post for the siege on the 30th floor.

The front page of last night's final edition of the Press was instrumental in the decision of Ashby Leach to give himself up according to Charles McKinnon, special agent in charge of the FBI office here. McKinnon said the page, prominently displaying the demands made by Leach was shown to Leach soon after the edition came off the presses "and helped convince him that he would get fair treatment."

When we got on the scene my sergeant told me to take my 30.06 and go into the president's office which was adjacent to where the suspect was holding the hostages. I got situated behind a large sofa. From there I could see the entire area of the main office and the movement of the suspect which I reported to the officer in charge.

After spending an hour or two in the office the lieutenant in charge of the tactical unit showed up and saw me lying behind the sofa. He almost had a heart attack. He said, "Who told that man to go into that office. Get him out of there now!" Normally the sergeant on the scene of any hostage situation was in charge of the operation, but seeing how this one was such a high profile media situation all of the brass decided to join in on the fun. Maybe they could get a little credit for ending the standoff. If things went bad they would be gone in a flash. But anyway I was ordered out of the office. Now there was no one to monitor the suspect's movements.

In the afternoon, after the daily paper came out and the suspect saw his demands were announced, he gave himself up. My partner and I placed him under arrest. When we got into the elevator we were swarmed by high ranking police personnel who took the prisoner away from us. When they got down to the ground floor, a large number of media were waiting for them. All of the brass got their pictures in the paper as if they had made the arrest.

Fatal End to Car Chase

I remember a car chase in the Fifth District where a zone car was in pursuit of a stolen auto. This chase lasted quite a while and finally ended at East 55th Street and Quincy where it was involved in an accident. The suspect hit a car broadside and caused a lot of front end damage. We weren't on the scene immediately but got there soon after. The sight I witnessed was something I could do without. The stolen auto caught fire after the collision and the driver got out without a scratch, but the female passenger wasn't so lucky. Her legs were pinned under the dash board, and she was unable to get out. When we got on the scene, the entire car was on fire and there was absolutely nothing that could be done for this poor girl. She was fully awake when the flames engulfed her, and you could hear her screaming for her life. It's something that is pretty hard to forget.

Slain Off-Duty Police Officer

In 1976 I read a news account of the death of one of my police academy friends, Mel Carter. I had gotten to know Mel pretty well. He was the kind of guy you could rely on for anything and who you wanted to cover your back in a dangerous situation. It was a shock to pick up the paper and read the following article.

The Cleveland Press

1976

A 29-year-old Cleveland policeman was found shot to death early today near a snow bank next to a parking lot at North Welsh Woods in the Euclid Creek Metro Park Reservation.

The policeman, Patrolman Melvin Carter, had been shot three times, at least once in the head.

Cleveland homicide detectives, Euclid Police and Metro parks rangers converged at the slaying scene. Euclid Creek Parkway, running through the area was blocked off until policemen could search the wooded spot for clues.

Ranger Chief James Johnson said the body was found after 2 A.M. by a young couple who had driven into the parking area.

Police said no vehicles were found in the area but after daybreak blood was found near where the body was discovered.

This indicated, police said, that Carter was killed on the spot—either kidnapped and driven there for execution or lured into meeting someone in the park.

Carter was dressed in civilian clothing. It was not certain if he was on duty.

There was no identification in his clothing and no money, only some keys. One key bore the insignia of the Cleveland Police Department. His watch was on his wrist.

Police said Carter worked from 8 A.M. to 4 P.M. yesterday in the Fourth District, Cleveland's Southeast Side.

Carter's car could not be located so Euclid Police put out an area-wide broadcast shortly after 8 A.M. for help in finding it.

Euclid police took the victim to University Hospital where he was pronounced dead.

He was still unidentified when taken to the county morgue. Some Cleveland policemen, at the morgue on an unrelated case, recognized him.

One bullet passed through Carter's head. It appeared a heavy-caliber handgun was used, police said.

Police said the killer or killers may have stripped the body of identification. However, it was pointed out, the patrolman may have been assigned to undercover work without any papers.

After reading the above article and talking to other officers it seems another officer, Patrolman Ardie Lightner and Carter's former wife, Beverly were being charged with his murder. Apparently Mel had shown up at his ex-wife's apartment as Ardie was leaving. According to his wife, there

65

was a struggle between the two and a shot was fired. Ardie said he was going to take Carter to the hospital. Later Lightner returned to the apartment and told Carter's ex-wife that he had died on the way to the hospital and he had dumped the body in the park.

Mrs. Carter had already told the detectives that she had picked up the gun and put it in Carter's car. After hearing of his death, Mrs. Carter took Carter's car and moved it to another location. The gun never was found.

According to the paper, the examiner, Dr. Hirsch, said the head wounds were inflicted from a distance of about three feet and the abdomen wound was inflicted with the barrel of the gun pressed against Carter's belt. He stated that the initial shot did not kill him.

Lightner was arrested at Kaiser Foundation Hospital with injuries he claimed he received from three men who attacked and robbed him. When he was arrested and told about the slaying of his friend Patrolman Carter. His reaction was of shock, "I'll be damned. That just ruined my whole day. He and I were friends. He was a good cop."

The next day the paper had the following article:

Cleveland Press December 1976

As police reconstruct events, Carter left his apartment on Cliff View Road at about 11:30 P.M. Monday. It was his habit to go out late at night and buy a newspaper. He lived only a few blocks from his ex-wife's apartment. They were divorced last spring.
Police believe Carter drove by her apartment and either saw Lightner's auto out front or decided to stop in.

66

Mrs. Carter said that Carter came to her door as Lightner was leaving. There were words, a fight and a shot was fired. She further stated that Lightner dragged Carter out of her apartment. She didn't know whether he was alive or dead. She said that she then disposed of Carter's auto by driving it away and parking it in front of 779 East 131st Street, north of St. Clair Avenue. Police had been looking for it yesterday and found it last night after an anonymous phone call.

Mrs. Carter said she was too frightened to call police after she returned to her suite. Police alleged that Lightner drove to the North Welsh Woods area in the Euclid Creek Metro Park Reservation. They said at that spot he may have "finished" the victim by firing two more shots.

So far police have only said that a possible motive for the killing on Carter may have been a romantic triangle situation.

When Mel was killed, it was a total blow to my mind because he was such a great guy. Finding out that he had been killed by another police officer was a double jolt. Lightner was the City Council President's driver at the time. Worse still, his wife had assisted in the crime by driving his car away from the scene and dumping it at another street. I think Mel would have been the first one from our academy class to get promoted.

His body was identified by two homicide detectives at the county morgue who recognized a distinctive key from the property of the deceased that only police officers had. If it wasn't for that fluke, who knows how long it would have taken to figure out who this man was.

CHAPTER 6

Community Response Unit
1979

Prelude to S.W.A.T

In 1979 after the Impact Tack Force Unit and the Tactical Unit had been dissolved, the city decided to start up a program geared to the needs of the community. This program was going to incorporate all aspects of police work from traffic enforcement to family fights, hostage negotiations and handling all other major crimes. They took personnel from all over the city and from every unit in the police department.

Since a lot of us were from the old Tactical Unit we would be known as the Tactical section of the Community Response Unit. We would work the whole city unlike with the Impact Tack force and the Tactical Unit. There were about 30 of us including females and minorities which was a big thing back then. We would be assigned districts to work and permanent partners.

I had just become a Christian a few years earlier and had shared my beliefs with whomever I worked with. It was no secret about where I stood and where I was coming from. Little did I know that this might become a problem with this new unit.

After the Tactical Unit had been disbanded I moved over to the Fifth District. I had been assigned a different partner from the one I had been working with the past few years. This guy knew that I was a Christian and apparently told the supervisors in charge of forming this new unit. My previous partner told me the secular image of a Christian is as a very passive, meek and mild individual who is unable to respond with deadly force if necessary.

When I found out I wasn't too happy with the individual that had started this problem. It hurt me to think that after working with me for a year and a half, he would have such a misconception of me.

Fortunately, when the time came to pick the members of this unit, I was included. On top of that I was chosen to be one of the unit's snipers which meant that my only job would be shooting.

We had about 30 members when we started the unit and were divided into two shifts. A short time after getting started we had three officers come in from the Los Angeles S.W.A.T. for hands-on training. We were all going to get the same training from these officers for about two weeks. It happened to be in the middle of winter and for these California boys this weather was quite a shock to the system. They taught us how to search buildings, houses and warehouses. We were also instructed on how to make a safe traffic stop involving dangerous suspects and how to search a person without putting yourself in danger. The L.A. S.W.A.T. Unit had a P.T. test which consisted of 20 pull ups,

50 pushups, 80 sit-ups in two minutes and a three mile run every three months or four times a year. Each event was worth a maximum of 100 points for a total of 400 points. To pass you needed a minimum of 221 points. To max the run you needed to complete the three miles in 18 minutes and then start subtracting points after that.

When the test became mandatory, we started losing people left and right because they were unable to pass. We felt that in order to face the rigors of the job we had to be in the best shape possible. The Lord blessed me with good physical abilities so after a few months I could max out the first three events which gave me 300 points going into the run.

We had the opportunity to work-out two hours a day in order to prepare for this test that we took every three months. A few of the guys didn't take advantage of this perk, but most did. I had always been thin so I figured that since I could work-out on duty, I would be able to put on some body weight.

I started slowly and over time increased the amount of time and weight that I spent each week. My goal was to have at least 200 pounds of body weight and bench press 300 pounds. There are many reasons that it's a good idea to work out regularly, but one of the most important is that when we go to a call up we can be there an hour or days without sleep or food. The better shape you're in, the more your body can handle.

Over a period of time I started to gain a little weight, and my weight lifting started to increase also. Now you have to remember that I was 36 years old when I started this and had never worked out on regular basis except for the three months that I spent in basic training in the Army. I would put in about eight hours a week of training. This was two hours, four days a week of very heavy weights. After about three years I was close to 200 pounds in body weight. I just kept on going never giving up. Then I broke the 200 mark and continued on to about 210 pounds. Now I started out at 175 pounds so to me this was great. The problem was that I hated to work my legs so most of this weight was in my upper body area.

I ended up bench pressing 300 pounds and dead lifting 425 pounds. I was pretty happy about my progress. I found out when you're working out you never compare yourself with anyone else because it doesn't matter how much you lift there's someone that'll come along and lift more.

One day I was in the gym working out as usual when this big guy came in. When I say big, I mean big! He had to weigh over 300 pounds of solid muscle and stood 6' 8". I was doing my usual weight of over 300 pounds when he came over and asked if he could use the weights when I was finished with them. I said, "Sure," and I continued for a couple of minutes more before saying he could have them. He walked over, picked up the 300 pounds and started to arm curl the bar. Now this was without warming up which I guess was his warm up weight. Talk about an ego deflator, this was it. I also saw him do an incline bench press with over 400 pounds which also was just for warm up.

Later on in my career when I was in the Aviation Unit I was assigned to attend career day at an elementary school on the west side. While there I ran across this big guy from the gym, who I had gotten to know as CJ and invited him for a helicopter ride. This turned out to be a potentially bad decision. As I started the engine and engaged rotor blades, I pulled up on the collective which gave us lift. As the helicopter started to lift off the ground, it also started to tilt toward his side. The more it tilted, the more I countered by applying left cyclic. By the time I was off the ground, I just about ran out of stick. As we hovered around we had about a 40 degree list to the right. What a sight!

Unfortunately, a few years after I retired I heard that he had died of a massive heart attack where his heart just exploded. He was only 30 years old. What a shame!

CHAPTER 7

S.W.A.T. Unit

1979 – 1988

Apprehending a fugitive wanted for Robbery - Homicide.
Youngstown, Ohio, January, 1986

The city purchased the armored vehicle in 1970, one of two made after the riots in the 1960's. The truck, affectionately known as "mother" because she was there to protect us, weighed 38,000 pounds with hardened rubber tires. It was initially designed to be a rescue and command vehicle and had a trap door in the rear in the event of an officer down. We could back over him, open the door, jump down and pull him inside. There were gun ports with steel plate covers for the windows which were also bullet proof. The trick was that with all of the plates down we were limited to a couple of slits for driving. Maneuvering this very heavy vehicle with poor visibility could be a little dangerous for the citizens.

Training

When we started the S.W.A.T. Unit there were just a handful in the country. Los Angeles was the best at the time. After getting our initial start from them, we continued training ourselves with shooting, building searches and repelling.

We trained constantly for several months perfecting our new found skills. As a sniper, I was issued a 30.06 cal. bolt action rifle with a 12 power scope. This is a big gun. We had several old timers on the department that were experienced shooters and several of us trained with them for a couple of weeks. Then we would go down to the range once or twice a week to practice. The first week I was there every day shooting all day long. Like I said this is a big gun and after a week of shooting my shoulder turned black and blue. It got so bad that the blood under the skin flowed down to my elbow discoloring half my arm. It looked worse than it was.

After adjusting the scope several times, we knew exactly where the round was going to hit. We got so good that we would place a three inch clay pigeon on the side of the cliff and consistently hit them at over 250 yards or more than 750 feet away. No brag just fact as they say.

We also had to be proficient with our hand guns. We built an obstacle course that we would run through using live fire. To me it was like playing cops and robbers only real life and death situations. In an urban area like Cleveland the chances were that we would never have to take a shot from more than a couple hundred feet at the most.

First S.W.A.T. Trainees

Comrades in Training 1986

S.W.A.T. Training Sessions

Close to Graduation

First Cleveland S.W.A.T. Team Members

Shooting On Hayden Avenue

One night we were called out at about 2:00 A.M. This was referred to as a "call up." Police radio had all of our pagers and home phone numbers and went down the list notifying everyone. We only worked days and afternoons so after midnight the unit would have to be called from home.

On one particular night a zone car was apparently called to an apartment in the Sixth District for shots being fired. When they arrived on the scene, they were met by people from the neighborhood and were informed that in the front apartment an elderly mentally unstable female lived by herself. She had a history of yelling at the kids and creating other problems for her neighbors.

This night she lost control and started shooting a hand gun at the children on the street because they were making too much noise for her. The first zone car called for the supervisor after several failed attempts to talk to her. The supervisor on the scene decided that if this woman had a gun and was unstable, it was best to play it safe and call the S.W.A.T. Unit to handle the situation.

S.O.P. (standard operating procedure) was that if the call up was on the east side of town, members living on the west side would stop at the Justice Center down town and pick up the equipment and "Mother" and bring them to the scene We did the reverse if it was on the west side. Each member of the team carried his own equipment such as bullet proof vests, weapons, gas masks, etc. in a large duffel bag which he kept with him at all times. This night the call up was on the east side of town, and I lived on the west side so I stopped at the J.C. to get the equipment. Since I was one of the snipers, I would ride inside of Mother along with a sergeant and a spotter.

When we arrived on the scene, we were told to pull up in front of the apartment for a clear view of the suspect's windows and door. Some members were already on the scene, and all attempts with negotiation had resulted in no response. After several hours it was decided to get an entry team set up and go into the apartment which was located on the second floor. My job as a sniper was to use deadly force if necessary. We had Sergeant O'Brien and two other officers not including myself in Mother.

I was ordered to shoot tear gas into the apartment in an attempt to drive her out onto the balcony so the entry team could enter without too much danger. We had 37 mm tear gas canisters that were designed to penetrate windows and doors. It's essential to know exactly where to aim the weapon as I found out the hard way back in the Fifth District. The trick was to aim at the lower part of the window because the projectile has a tendency to climb in flight. After I shot several canisters through the glass doors the suspect came charging out onto the balcony and dropped to the floor of the porch. We were no more than 50 feet from the apartment so for reasons unknown to me, I was told that if I had to take a shot to use the 30 cal. carbine instead of my 30.06. Apparently this was too much force to use on an elderly woman and the city did not want bad publicity. This did not make any sense to me at all because if you have an armed suspect threatening citizens or the police, what did it matter whether it was a 6'8" 260 pound male or a small female? Well as they train you in the military, you follow orders and ask questions later. One problem with using the carbine was that it had a peep sight instead of a scope. In the dark it was literally impossible to get a sight picture. The only way was to point and shoot and hope that you hit your target.

This all might sound cold and harsh but the reality is that there are people out there that are a danger to society.

Because we are the arm of the government which was created by the Lord, it's our duty to eliminate that danger.

The government is just one of three institutions the Lord God ordained. The others are the Family Unit, and the Church, which is the Bride of Christ.

After the suspect came out onto the porch, the entry team decided to enter the apartment. I was looking out through a gun port from the armed truck but really couldn't see the suspect too well because of the darkness. The only light was from the street lights. When the front door was kicked in, the suspect heard the noise and while she was seated, she raised her right hand. At this time my spotter yelled that she had a gun. In that split second an image flashed through my head of one of my co-workers coming through the door and being shot. So I did what I was trained to do. I took the shot which hit her in the upper part of her torso and knocked her back down. She started to get back up, and I shot her again. By this time the entry team was in the apartment.

A little back story that I found out later was the first officer in stumbled over a coffee table in the middle of the room and went down. The second officer in seeing the officer down assumed that he had been shot and ran over to where the suspect was and shot her three more times. As it turned out, the female was a heavy set person and most of the hits from the bullets entered the fatty parts of her body so she wasn't seriously hurt.

This was my first but not last taste of what it's like to be on an adrenaline high. After all was said and done I started to shake. I had no idea why but found out that this is what happens when coming down from all the adrenaline. We had to turn in our weapons and file reports and were off work for three days while we got checked out by a doctor to make sure we were not affected by the traumatic experience. It might sound callous but I just saw this as my job. It was a matter of whether she was going to be hurt or one of the officers.

The following is an official Police Department Information report typed by Officer David Child who was my spotter:

Sir,

Reported for duty on 6-5-86, at 1700 hrs. and assigned to the S.W.A.T. Unit. At 1745 hrs. received a phone call from police radio of a barricaded female at 1745 Hayden Ave. apt. #1 with shots fired. PTL Murtaugh #91, PTL. Albright #497 and I were assigned to 9114 (which is the 38 thousand pound armed vehicle) for front cover. At 2100 hours I observed the female suspect light some object or paper on fire. At this time PTL Murtaugh notified CFD, who responded to the scene. At 2115 hrs. The female broke two small windows in the front porch door and then exited the door and sat down on the porch floor. The Entry Team asked if she had a weapon. We responded that we could not see her right hand. I used the P.A. on 9114 and ordered the female to put her hands on top of her head. At approximately 2117 hrs. the Entry Team entered the apartment and the female turned and fired several shots at the members of the Entry Team from a weapon she was holding. At this time fearing for the Entry Teams' Life, PTL. Albright then fired one round at the suspect. She fell onto her back and raised her weapon again, and PTL. Albright fired one more time at the suspect, using the .30 cal. M-1 carbine, Plainfield SN.346174. This weapon is assigned to Car 9114. He then stopped firing due to the fact the Entry Team was entering the porch area. At no time during

84

the event did PTL. Murtaugh or I fire any shots from 9114.

Arrested: Verna Jackson 41 BFS of 1147 Hayden Ave, Apt #1

Phone # 249-1544, DOB of   The above female was conveyed from the scene by EMS #12, to Huron Rd. Hosp. where this female was treated and confined, detail established by Sixth Dist.

Every officer asks himself, whether or not he admits it, if he can use "deadly force." We all train for such an event and practice all of the time at the range. We go through scenarios on when to shoot, but until that time actually comes no one knows for sure whether he has what it takes. Sure people can say, "Of course I can," but deep down they really don't know. It's the same question even in combat. The soldier wonders whether or not he can pull the trigger. I felt good about myself not because I had to shoot someone, but because I did my job and answered the biggest question any officer or soldier can ask. It's never a good thing when it comes to that, but the Lord created government and we are the enforcers of the laws of that government.

Canoeing

My brushes with death didn't always come with the job. There was a time in1984 I had gotten some time off work and was invited to go canoeing with a friend of mine from church. My two sons were invited to come along to do a father/son thing. I've never been canoeing before, but it sounded like fun and I'm always up for new adventures.

The place where we were going was about a two hour drive from home.

The place was owned by a former Cleveland Browns player who rented canoes and other recreational vehicles. This was my first time doing anything like this so I didn't know what to expect. We rented two canoes. I wasn't really dressed properly for this activity because I was wearing a shirt with blue jeans and cowboy boots. I don't know why we weren't provided life preservers or any other safety equipment.

My oldest son got into the canoe with my friend; his brother got into the canoe with me. We started down the river going at an easy pace with everyone rowing. The trip was about two or three miles downriver so it was going to take about an hour and a half to two hours depending on how fast we traveled.

It turned out to be a great trip. We saw things from a different prospective and communed with nature. When we got to the area where we were supposed to be picked up, my eldest started playing around which was his nature. He started charging us trying to ram our canoe with his. Now canoes are not that stable because they are so narrow. So when he finally hit us broadside, we tipped over. Both my son and I landed in the water. Like I said earlier we had no life preservers or any other safety device on. When we hit the water, clothes and boots filled with water. I sank like a rock. The water was probably 10 feet deep and I'm 6'2" so I had almost 4 feet of water over my head. I don't remember much about how I got out, but I do remember struggling with all my might trying to get my head above the water. With my boots filled with water and my clothes soaked, it was like I had an anchor weighing me down. After several moments of panic I made it to the bank of the river. My struggle was still not over since the bank was muddy and went straight up about four feet. When I got there, I still couldn't get out. I finally clawed my way up the bank looking like a drowned rat I'm sure. When I got out, the van was there to pick me up. I was more embarrassed than anything else because I didn't want to admit I was in trouble and had almost drowned.

We got back to the car. I had forgotten completely about my son and how he made it to shore. I was wet and cold and just wanted to get dry. To this day I have no idea how I got to the surface, how I got out of the river and how I climbed up that muddy bank. Why there was no safety equipment issued or why we didn't ask for any are a mystery to me.

It would have been so easy to have drowned and be fished out of the river downstream somewhere. Once again "Boy was I lucky." After about the fifth time no matter how dense someone is, you have to start to think that maybe the Lord is trying to tell you something like, get your act together. He'd showed me how easy it was for Him to take my life.

Part Time at the Go-Kart Track

During my career as a police officer I probably worked at least a hundred different part-time jobs. One of these jobs was working at a go-kart track. I worked there for about six years. This was one of the worst jobs that I had. The worst was working at the Greyhound Bus Station. I worked there for about three years, and every time I walked through the front door my stomach would start to churn because I knew that the potential for trouble was on a very high scale. There were local derelicts and derelicts arriving from all over the country. The reason that they hired off-duty police officers was because when they had unarmed security guards, one had his throat slit wide open by one of the transients coming through town. The security office had dried blood all over the door frame and walls from previous incidents over the years.

I started working part-time jobs because the pay on the department was so low at the time we were just above poverty level. In 1969 I was making $6,000 a year. After a while you start to rely on the extra money to pay your bills. Then you would get another part-time job for the extra money that you needed because you were paying off bills. I got into the vicious cycle. There were so many jobs available that you had your choice. Of course, the worst ones paid the most.

I had been in the S.W.A.T. Unit for about four or five years at the time and had been working out on a regular base. I had also been taking karate lessons for about two years so I was in pretty good shape.

I was working at the track one night as usual. I worked from early evening to closing time which was about 12:00 midnight. My job was to take care of any trouble makers on the track. One of the rules was that there was no bumping or crashing into each other. Violators were thrown off the track without a refund.

About 8:30 P.M. there were some young guys that started to get out of control by cutting each other off and slamming into each other. The employees yelled for them to get off, but they kept on going. Finally, one of the employees threw a tire at them to stop them. After some time the trouble makers came in. I told them to get off the track and to leave the property and not come back. This one guy couldn't have been much bigger than 5'9", 165 pounds. He came up to me demanding his money back because he didn't get his full ride. I told him that he wouldn't get his money back because the rules clearly stated that you don't ram each other. He got all irate and wanted to know when I got off duty because he was coming back to kick my butt. I told him and he went on his way.

I didn't think too much more about it. At midnight we closed up. I was in my car driving out of the parking lot when the same guy came flying into the parking lot and cut me off preventing me from leaving. He jumped out of his car and came running up to me pointing his finger at me and said, "I told you I'd be back. Another cop got in my face and I got his badge." I thought to myself that he's either crazy or he's a black belt or something, because you can't be in your right mind to challenge a police officer in uniform to a fight. Yet this is what he was doing. I got out of my car and I looked at him and said, "This is how it's going to be. If you kick my butt, you're going to jail. If I kick your butt, you're going to jail. So whatever happens, you're going to go to jail. Do you understand?" He said, "Let's get it on."

I didn't want to be brawling out in the middle of the parking lot so I told him, "Let's go behind the building." When we got back there he took off his hat and placed it on the ground next to him. This act tells me that he was really serious. I grabbed his pony tail pulling him down to the ground backward; he hit the ground on his back. I came down on top of him with my knee in his chest. I punched him in the face and after a few swings, he yelled he just wanted to talk. Talk was over with. I put the handcuffs on him, dragged him into the office and called for a zone car to convey him to the district for booking. I was charging him with assault on a police officer.

The conveying officers arrived and when told what he was charged with, had a good talk with him about the error of his ways. When he was conveyed downtown in the early morning hours, he was again given a good talking to. Come to find out that he wasn't a black belt in anything, just crazy.

Galleria Attempted Purse Snatching

I worked a part-time job at a high priced shopping mall called The Galleria. It had two levels with about 20 or so stores with a food court in the middle. I would just walk around stopping in the various stores talking to the employees just letting them know that I was around. I would normally work anywhere from six to eight hours per shift. On a normal day there was nothing to do so I would end up in the book store looking through the different books. That would kill an hour or so. I enjoy reading, so it was a pleasure. If I did get a call, it was usually for a shop lifter at one of the stores. I would respond, make the arrest, complete the reports for the store owners and take the thief to jail. It was not too hard of a job. Not like the Grey Hound bus station, or the Go-kart track.

One day, my wife came to visit me and do a little shopping at the mall. I was in my favorite store when she arrived and asked me to come up to this particular women's clothing store. I told her that I'd be right up. She left the book store and went back to the clothing store. I followed two or three minutes behind her. Now just so that you know, I worked in uniform because that's why the owners paid us. The presence of a uniformed officer would alleviate problems.

As I got to the clothing store, I turned the corner and immediately noticed a young male coming from the back of the store walking at a fast pace toward my wife. In a second or two I could see what was happening. My wife was carrying her purse over her shoulder and wasn't looking around. As soon as he saw me, he did an immediate about-face and started walking back to the rear of the store. That told me he was a second away from snatching her purse. It didn't take a genius to figure that out. Number one what were two young males doing in a women's store; number two he almost made a run toward my wife and number three as soon as he saw me, he turned around and hightailed to the back of the store.

Something snapped in my head and primal instinct took over. I saw a predator about to attack my wife, and the only thing that I had on my mind was to protect her. I think my blood pressure went through the roof, and I called them out of the store to have a talk with them. I noticed several large garbage bags in the back full of clothes that they were going to steal. That would have been impossible to prove. When they got out of ear shot of anyone else, I told them that this is their lucky day. I was so upset that I was shaking but I put on a calm and cool facade. I said "That woman is my wife, and I know that you were going to steal her purse. If you had touched her, I would have shot you. So, as I said, count this as your lucky day."

I ran a want and warrant check on them both and it came back negative. Since I had nothing else on them, I cut them loose. I really don't know what I would have done if the theft had indeed taken place and I was there to witness it, but fortunately it didn't come to that.

Motorcycle Chase

We were detailed to the downtown area because of a big event, and it was our job to respond to any disturbance. I was working with my regular partner, and I was driving. As I stated before, I hated to do reports, and he disliked driving. A perfect fit. This was an all-day event, so it was going to pay over time.

We heard over the radio that one of our cars was attempting to stop a motorcycle for a traffic violation and he took off on them. They lost him around the Cleveland Stadium by the lake front.

Just as we got to the area, he suddenly sped by us. I have to confess at this point that I had gotten to be an adrenaline junkie, or maybe I have always been a bit crazy and liked speed. So when he sped away, I thought, "Here we go; I'm not going to lose this guy." We chased him through the downtown area, up and down the side streets. Finally, he headed across the Detroit Superior Bridge at a high rate of speed. When he got on the other side, he turned left onto West 25th Street. He was riding a fairly small bike, probably a 350 cc but still was going at a good rate. We were driving Dodges at the time which were small but quick, so I had no problem keeping up with him. At one point I had gotten next to him and could have nudged him into the curb, but I figured this was just a traffic violation and did not warrant serious physical harm. So we just followed him until we were approaching a busy intersection at West 25th and Lorain.

The way this guy was driving he had to be high on something. As we approached the intersection, he wasn't slowing down any. We were traveling about 60 to 70 M.P.H., and I figured that if by chance he did make it through I didn't want to slow down too much and lose him. I kept my speed up and just before entering the intersection, he laid the bike down on the left side and started to slide while staying with the bike. As he was sliding, the back tire of the motorcycle struck a tire of a parked car thus flipping the motorcycle and launching its driver through the air. He must have flown at least 75 feet. I had my eyes glued on this mesmerizing flying object. He landed in the middle of the intersection and was fortunate not to be hit by a car. When he landed, I regained my senses still traveling at over 60 MPH. I saw two lanes of traffic coming from the opposite direction and two lanes of stopped traffic in my direction. That left few options: lock up the brakes and hope for the best.

Time slowed way down. I had experienced this phenomenon before and would again. It was like watching a movie in slow motion. I started to slide toward the stopped car in front of me, and as we slid I could see that car getting bigger and bigger. Just before we hit I said those famous words that you never want to hear from people in control of a vehicle you're riding in, "Oh Crap!" As we struck the car's rear end, I could see the hood of my car fold up on itself. Steam was coming from the front end. It all happened in slow motion, and I was not conscious of any impact when we hit the car.

I jumped out and ran to check on the driver of the car I hit. My partner ran into the intersection to check on the driver of the motorcycle knowing that he had to be dead. No one can slide into a parked car, fly through the air more than 75 feet and crash down onto the roadway without being killed.

The driver of the car that I hit was a young female about 19 or 20 years old. Although she stated that she was fine, I was concerned she might be injured but unaware of it at the moment. So I asked her several more times to make sure and each time she said she was fine.

My partner in the mean-time had checked on the rider of the motorcycle and had called for assistance with traffic control and to take any injured to the hospital. To his total surprise he found the cyclist was conscious and alert and had only minor injuries. This was probably due to the fact that he was drunk and high on drugs. As the old saying goes "The Lord looks out for morons and drunks." I'm just being facetious. He was taken to the nearest hospital along with a police escort to make sure he didn't leave without a few traffic citations. Also the mother of the girl that I hit arrived on the scene with pen and paper in hand. I thought to myself this is not good. It was no mystery what she had in mind. She started getting all of the information so that she could sue the city and anyone else involved. It took several years, but the city did settle a law suit for a few thousand dollars.

In the meantime we went to the hospital to take care of business with this maniac that survived the accident. When we started to interview him, he started to swear up a blue streak calling us all kinds of names. Here I thought this guy was dead. After giving him several tickets, we left him to his own destructive devices.

As a foot note to this story the accident happened on a warm summer night, right in front of the local fire house where all of the firemen were sitting watching the traffic. They were right there to help any injured and to clean the roadway of debris. They sure got their money's worth that night.

Hijacking

On January 4, 1985, I was working part-time at the East Ohio Gas Company which I would do at least once a week. This was just another of many extra jobs I had over the years. The reason I started part time jobs was when driving to work one night I found my gas tank almost empty with only fifty cents in my pocket. From that day on I told myself this will never happen again. I probably worked a hundred different jobs over the next twenty-five years. The deals with these jobs were like an addiction. Once you start it's almost impossible to stop. The money was usually pretty good, but after a while I had to use it to pay bills. Then I had to add another job in order to have extra money.

I worked at the Gas Company for a total of 14 years. On this date I got a page to call police radio. Well there was no mystery about what they wanted. There was a female at Cleveland Hopkins Airport that had hijacked an airplane and was demanding to be flown to South America. I hurried over to the Justice Center to pick up one of our S.W.A.T. cars and any equipment that was needed. There was a problem as it was rush hour and with the traffic on the freeway it would take forever to get to the airport. Well a little problem like rush hour traffic wasn't going to stop me from getting there in a timely matter. When I hit the interstate, I also hit the outside berm. It's about 20 miles from downtown Cleveland and on a normal day maybe a 20 minute drive. During rush hour this could take at least twice that amount of time. Since I was on the berm with no other way to get around the traffic, I kicked it into high gear and got up to around 70 M.P.H. with red light and siren. I was going so fast that I was kicking up all of the debris on the side of the road.

When I got to the airport I was met by one of our sergeants who filled me in on the situation. Apparently this woman shot one of the guards at the entrance to Concourse C and ran down to one of the gates and forced her way onto the waiting airplane. The situation had been going on for an hour or so before I arrived. At this point the suspect had let most of the passengers off the plane. She still held hostage a young couple with a baby, an older couple and two other passengers. They were all located in the coach section of the plane, and the negotiator was attempting to talk to her from the plane's doorway.

I was told to take my 30.06 rifle and go to another ramp several exits down from the plane and set up at the end of the ramp so that I had a clean shot. I was also to keep the command post informed of her activity.

I got situated at the end of the ramp about 200 feet from the plane. Looking through the scope I could see into the plane and identify the suspect and the passengers. All of the passengers were sitting in their seats, and the female suspect was moving around. While normally it would be no problem taking a shot from that distance, the fact that these airliners have double windows gave me concern that the bullet might be deflected as it entered the aircraft. I had never tested this theory in practice so it was an unknown factor.

Normally I would have a spotter with me so that I would not have to keep looking through the scope and could rest my position every once in a while. Due to the cold which was somewhere around 15 degrees, I started to cramp up after being in one position for hours. This could be dangerous especially because I had to maintain readiness. If I had to take the shot, I would get the order without much warning. I continued looking and reporting to the command of the suspect's activity.

After several hours they decided on a plan to open the back ramp to distract her while the main entry team would enter from the front. There are curtains between the first class and coach section of the plane. The entry team was unable to see the suspect, so I would have to continue to update on her activity.

When the rear door opened and the suspect heard the noise, she fell to the floor with her back to the bulkhead between the seats. The plan was that when the rear door opened the suspect would turn facing the back of the plane and the entry team would enter from the front. The first officer would go in without anything in his hands because he was planning on grabbing her from behind and subduing her.

As the team entered, the first officer who was unarmed located the suspect between the seats and was shot in the chest. The second officer heard the shot, reached around the first officer and shot the suspect point blank in the chest disabling her enough to grab the gun from her.

Several months prior to this we had practiced making entries into 727's provided by United Airlines. So it was unreal to think that here we were actually involved in a real hijacking situation. At the time we managed to get six men into the plane in less than six seconds. Each man had a position to take covering the cabin, the first class and the coach area. We were all familiar with this scenario.

The passengers were hustled out of the plane through the rear and the suspect was subdued. EMS was called in to attend to the officer that was shot in the chest and the suspect's wounds. Fortunately, the officer was wearing a bullet proof vest and the suspect shot him with a small 22 caliber hand gun. He had minor injuries while the suspect actually had to be resuscitated after her heart stopped. She was taken to the hospital where she was treated and eventually taken to jail. The woman had severe mental problems and was turned over to the mental ward of the hospital.

The entire episode lasted about eight hours and then back to the J.C. for reports and all of the other necessities that were required after a shooting. I finally got home sometime in the early morning.

The Hanging

We got a call up shortly after getting home from work around midnight which is usually the case. You just get into bed and the phone rings and you know who and what it is. The information that I got from police radio was that a black male forced his way into an eastside hospital and kidnapped his girlfriend at gun point.

I got dressed and made my way down to the Justice Center to pick up equipment that we might need on the scene. The location was on the far southeast side of town, so it took us some time to get there.

Upon arrival we met with the S.W.A.T. supervisor, Sergeant Horan, to get a briefing and our assignments. We were told that several attempts had been made to contact the suspect with no response and that the victim's and suspect's cars were in the garage, so it was pretty evident that they were both still there. After several more unsuccessful tries to make contact, it was decided to make an entry into the house. This is where things started to get moving. My heart started racing and the adrenaline began to flow because I knew this guy was armed and dangerous and he knew we were here. We had no idea where he was, so he had the advantage.

We had a four man entry team including my partner, Sergeant Horan, another officer and me. We entered through the attached garage and noticed the victim's purse inside her car. This almost confirmed that she was in the house. It was about 3:30 A.M. and the house was deadly quite. We moved slowly into the kitchen from the garage trying to be as quite as possible. The house was completely dark except for a light in the living room which was the next room off the kitchen. The only thing we heard was an eerie silence.

We crept toward the living room still trying to pick up on any sound at all. Then we turned the corner and were taken aback by what we saw. Here were two bodies hanging from the ceiling. Both obviously had been dead for some time. We still had the rest of the house to secure, but it was difficult to take your eyes off the scene of death. We continued through the rest of the house and when it was secure, we called in the homicide detectives.

It appears that after the suspect kidnapped his girlfriend from the hospital, he brought her home. He must have been planning this for some time because of all of the work that went into carrying out the murder suicide. He had screwed two eye bolts into the ceiling beam and attached the rope to each. He then tied his girlfriend's hands behind her and stood her up on a table top where he placed the rope around her neck. Then at some point he knocked the table out from under her, and she strangled to death. The next thing he did was to get up on another end table and place the other rope around his neck and kick the table out from under his feet thus hanging himself.

The girlfriend's body was just a couple of feet off the floor while his feet were actually touching the floor. Also there was a hand gun at his feet where he had dropped it after dying. You have heard the phase that when a person is hanged its "stretching the neck." Well let me tell you that it actually does stretch the neck to about twice the normal length. How or why I couldn't tell you. I just know that it does.

Now this was definitely not my first homicide and I had been on the police department many years by this time, but for some reason these deaths affected me differently.

Normally on the job you see things that most people don't see and you kind of shove it to the back of your brain so you don't think about it. If you dwelled on it, you would not be able to do your job. But when I got home after this and lay down to go to sleep, it was about 7:00 A.M. I just laid there thinking about that poor girl just hanging there, her life gone. She was a pretty white woman in her late 20's or early 30's. What really affected me the most was the eerie silence in the house followed by the sight of two dead bodies just hanging there. It wasn't the first bad scene that I'd been to and it sure wasn't the last, but it had spooked me.

Off Duty Officer Involved Standoff

We were just completing roll call on the first shift at the S.W.A.T. office when we were notified by police radio that there was an armed suspect in East Cleveland who had shot a security guard the night before. As it turned out the suspect was an off-duty Cleveland Police Officer. This was going to be different because it was one of our own.

It just so happened that the armored truck, "Mother," was in the shop for maintenance in Bedford Heights which is about a 30 minute ride from downtown on a good day. The City of East Cleveland was about 30 minutes in the other direction. The sergeant ordered my partner and me to go out there, pick up the truck, take it back to the J.C., equip it and get out to the scene as fast as possible. We picked up a marked police car and high tailed it out to the dealership.

It would be a good hour of driving, because this truck weighs 38,000 pounds and won't go over 55 M.P.H., plus we had to bring it back to the J.C. and equip it which would take another half an hour. You're talking a good two hours before we could get to the scene. We called the dealership ahead of time to make sure they'd have the truck ready when we got there. My partner would drive the truck this time, and I would drive the marked police car and run interference back to the J.C. and then again out to the scene.

When we got there, we met with the S.W.A.T. supervisor on the scene at the command post which was on another street away from the suspect's apartment. We were told to pull up in front of the apartment and take up position for a shot if need be. We were told the suspect had shot up the first cars that arrived on the scene earlier in the morning and refused to communicate with the on scene negotiator. We were also told that this is one of our own and not to shoot unless he leaves the building armed, per the Chief.

This was August and as the day went along the heat increased to around 90 degrees. The armored truck had no air conditioning. With all the doors closed and windows shut, it was almost unbearable inside. As we pulled up in front, I noticed that there were three East Cleveland police cars that had their overhead lights shot out and bullet holes in the side of the cars. As we came to a stop, I heard what sounded like rain drops hitting a tin roof, only these were bullets hitting the side of the truck. I could see through the gun ports that the suspect was firing at anything he saw. We had the entire block evacuated, so the only thing for him to shoot at were police vehicles. I noticed that the suspect was completely naked, and he started to set up tin cans on

102

the windowsill and started shooting. He continued to ignore any type of communications. As the time dragged on we opened the driver's door and the rear door to get a little fresh air, but kept the right side of the truck facing the suspect's apartment sealed up.

In the afternoon he started to light things on fire and tossed them out the window. He lit his police shirt and held it several minutes until it was going good and threw it out. He also threw cans, lights, cloths and anything else that he got hold of.

Then around 4:00 P.M., I noticed that he was trying to set a fire in the middle of the living room floor. Each time the fire would go out, he would relight it. He attempted this several more times until the fire caught and started to spread catching the drapes on fire. I couldn't see what he was lighting but it was now an inferno. I could see him on the floor crawling toward the kitchen area, but just before the kitchen he opened the closet door and crawled inside. I was told to shoot tear gas into the closet to try and drive him out into the open so that he could escape the fire. The gas cartridges called ferret rounds were shot from a 12 gauge shotgun. They were fairly accurate at a short distance and would penetrate thin plywood. I shot four rounds through the door, and in a couple of minutes I saw the door open and the suspect crawl toward the kitchen. An entry team was ready to go in when the word was given.

As we waited for him to vacate the apartment or give himself up, neither of which he did, the fire spread to the entire apartment. We were sure that no one could survive. The fire department was sent in to put out the fire. Once the fire was under control, the fire fighters entered the

103

apartment and discovered the suspect's charred remains in the hallway between the kitchen and the living room.

Stolen Highway Patrol Car

Early Sunday morning I received a call up in connection with a male suspect in his early 20's who had stolen a highway patrol police car the night before. It was located in the Second District. We responded to the scene and met with the sector supervisor. Apparently this situation had been going on for quite a while because there was a State Patrol Officer on the scene along with various other supervisors that normally wouldn't be there for a stolen police car. There was a lot of media coverage which may have been why all the bosses were there. Normally the more bosses at the location, the more messed up the situation is going to be. The old saying "Too many cooks spoil the soup."

Another thing that was unusual is that instead of setting up the command post away from the suspect's location, they were set up in the kitchen of the suspect's house. The suspect was up in the attic. Ideally, everyone should be away from where S.W.A.T. is set up, so that we are not distracted from our primary duties, protecting lives and capturing the suspect unharmed. The involvement of so many other law agencies just makes for confusion; something you don't need when dealing with life and death situations. This whole event was going to turn out badly.

It was decided to go up into the attic and try to take the suspect alive if possible. This was decided after talking with the suspect for several hours. About an hour or so later there was a gunshot, and no one heard from the suspect afterward.

The S.W.A.T. assigned four of us to enter the attic and check on the condition of the suspect. We knew this guy had a gun and knew that there was only one way we could come up the stairs, so he had all of the advantages. Nevertheless, we had to go up. There was no other way after spending hours trying to negotiate with no results. We would go up as we had practiced many times before. The stairway went half way up and then turned 180 degrees and continued the rest of the way. The first officer would advance carrying a shotgun. I would go next carrying a hand held mirror on an extension pole checking ahead of our movement. Two other officers would follow behind me for cover.

As we started up the stairs, I had the mirror out ahead of us so that I could look around the corner as we made the turn at the stair case. On the way up I noticed red gobs that looked like meat on the stairs but concentrated more on not getting shot. As we made the turn, I could see the top of the stairway. There was a two foot wall along the side of the opening in the attic. This wall blocked our view into the attic until we got almost to the top. I finally got up far enough to see over the top of the wall with the mirror, but I couldn't see the suspect anywhere. So we continued up.

Now let's stop and look at what's really happening here. Picture yourself going up a dark stairway in a strange house that you have never been in before looking for a crazy gunman with a shot gun who wants to hurt or kill you. But this is your job and is what the city pays you to do. As you get closer to the top of the stairway, you know that the suspect is up there hiding. He knows you're coming and is prepared, but there is no other option. You have to go. Talk about being on an adrenaline high. You can't imagine the feelings when you know that you might get shot or have to take someone else's life. Believe it or not at moments like this, I felt the most alive.

We finally got to the top after working our way up very slowly not taking any unnecessary risks. As we took a step to the left of the stairway, there was the suspect lying on his back with his head against the 2 foot wall lining the stairway opening, or I should say what was left of his head. Apparently he had placed this sawed off shotgun in his mouth and pulled the trigger taking off top of his head. The skin covering his skull was flapped in front of his face. The red pieces of meat that we saw coming up the stairs were his brains that flew out of his head when he was shot. It was a sight that I had seen before in my career.

Two Suicides

Suicide is one of the most common causes of death and statistics show that firearms are commonly involved. Suicide is not glamorous or the answer to problems. It's not quiet or clean. Most often it's pretty messy and can devastate the lives of the survivors, including family members, loved ones and friends. I recall one on a particularly cold, rainy day. We were riding around answering the calls given us by radio when we received an assignment to respond to a call of a male shot at an address on the near west side of the city.

Upon arrival at the scene, we walked up to the front door and were met by this hysterical young woman who was so distraught we really could not understand a word she was saying. In the living room we saw a male obviously dead, lying on the couch. We continued to get more information from this woman about what took place and checked to see if anyone else was injured. Next to the body was a hand gun. Clearly the victim's injuries were caused by gun shot. We could see parts of his skull, blood and brain matter spattered all over the walls and ceiling.

Eventually as we talked to the young woman, the events became clear. According to her, she and the victim were having a fight, and as the fight escalated, he reached under the couch and pulled out a .38 revolver. I imagined her fear thinking he was going to shoot her. Instead, he placed the gun in his mouth and pulled the trigger, killing himself.

His girlfriend told us that this was his way of getting back at her for their fight. I remember thinking what a waste of a young life. I can't imagine any situation that was so desperate as to end your life. The old saying about suicide is that it is a permanent solution for a temporary problem. The only conceivable explanation is the lack of HOPE. As long as you have hope, there is a light at the end of the tunnel. Without hope, there is nothing left.

I recollect another time while on the day shift, as a member of S.W.A.T., we received a call to respond to an address on the far west side of the city where there was a report of a man with a gun.

Normal procedure upon arrival is to set up a perimeter around the suspect's house and the Command Post at another location. The Command Post included S.W.A.T. Supervisors, District Supervisors and other personnel that could be of help. In accordance to the General Police Order, whenever the S.W.A.T. Unit is called up and we are on location, the ranking police officer is in command of the situation regardless of rank. This procedure leaves no question as to who is in charge with multiple supervisors on the scene.

There are four perimeter teams and each team member had a specific duty to perform. The outside cover team was assigned to the front and rear of the house to cover all of the exits. We normally put two men at one corner and two more at the opposite side. That way all four sides are covered and no matter what happens, these men are to never leave their position. The snipers are normally a two man team. One is the spotter, the other the shooter. My normal job was the shooter in the sniper team but this day I was assigned to the entry. The sniper team would find a location, normally a neighboring house with a second floor. They set up so that if the call came down they could either fire tear gas, or as a last resort, shoot with the rifle. When they can't find a house, they're stuck in a location outside and hopefully it's good weather. The door man is normally our biggest and strongest man. He's equipped with a large sledge hammer and a pry bar. We also have what is affectionately called "Jethro." This is a steel pipe about four feet long and eight inches across with handles on both sides. It is filled with lead and weighs about seventy pounds. If needed, two men would grab each side and forcefully slam it into the door until it comes down. Occasionally a door would not budge and in those cases have to use other means to gain entry.

The final team is the entry team. It is led by a S.W.A.T. sergeant and consisted of five officers. Each man has a specific assignment: the search team, the cover team and the prisoner team. At the Command Post the S.W.A.T. Lieutenant kept abreast of the situation and coordinated the teams around the perimeter.

As time went by there were multiple attempts to contact the suspect who turned out to be a distraught 17 year old male. He had come home from school, gone into his bedroom with a rifle and threatened to kill himself. Try as they may, his parents were unable to get through to him and finally called the police.

As the day wore on we were unable to make any kind of contact with him. We then approached the house with the entry team. As we concealed ourselves next to the side of the house for cover, we peeked into the front window to see if we could locate him. Hopefully, if we had to make an entry, we knew exactly where he was located. As we tried to observe the interior of the house, we saw a male lying on the front room floor. He wasn't moving. We notified the Command Post and were given the order to enter the residence.

As we entered the house which was unlocked, we started the search for anything that might pose a danger to us. We checked the suspect and observed that he had a single gunshot wound to the front of his chest. A rifle was lying on the floor next to him. There was no question that this was a self-inflicted gunshot wound. The Homicide Unit took over after we secured the entire house to insure that it was safe for anyone else to enter. We secured our equipment, left the scene and returned to the J.C. and reported off duty. The whole call up lasted about eight hours.

Channel 8's Standoff and Shooting

One December day we were called up and informed of a male in the main lobby of a local television station. He was reportedly holding two guns to his head demanding better treatment for veterans.

When we arrived, we could see the male standing in the lobby with both guns to his head. We entered from the rear of the building without being seen. There was no need for outside cover, as would be normal procedure in a case like this, because there was no way that he could escape. It was pretty close to zero degrees and since I was one of the snipers I would normally be outside somewhere with a vantage point on the suspect. I was relieved to find I didn't have to stand outside. I took up a position in the first office next to the lobby where the suspect was. I was told that if he in anyway made a threatening move towards any one, I was to take him out. This is something that is never an easy thing to do. Unfortunately, we live in a society of violent people and it's the law enforcement branch that is charged with the responsibility for dealing with them. I have trained for this job for years now and discovered that if it comes to a point where I would have to take a shot, I am able to. The incident on Woodworth Avenue where I had to shoot the woman in her apartment certainly proved that I was prepared to do what was necessary.

The standoff went on for several hours. The negotiator was getting nowhere with the male suspect. He was totally out of his mind and rambled about different things that made no sense. All of a sudden there were two muffled shots. We rushed into the lobby to find the suspect lying on the floor with two head wounds. Both guns went off only a fraction of second apart.

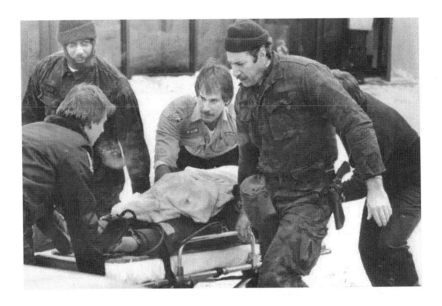

He lay there, and I could hear the gurgling sounds of dying coming from his throat. EMS rushed in, but there was little they could do. We carried him out into the waiting ambulance. He was conveyed to the nearest hospital where he was pronounced dead.

Hospital Operation

One day after roll call, my partner and I were detailed to the hospital to guard a prisoner that was arrested for burglary and theft. The suspect had apparently broken into a deli during the night to rob the place. This seemed like an easy job. Get in and out before the police arrived. Well the owner of the store had set up a booby trap. There was a shot gun under the counter facing up and out from the register. When the register was opened, the shot gun went off shooting the suspect in the face. After being shot he was still there lying on the floor with shotgun pellets in his face and head. He was placed under arrest and was taken to the hospital where he was placed under lock and key until he was operated on and recovered enough to be taken to jail. We were to guard him during the operation and were told we would have to put on hospital gowns, hats and the shoe covering to prevent static electricity. We both put the gowns over our uniforms and went out into the hall where the suspect was laying on a stretcher waiting for the operation.

Apparently, he had a pellet lodged in his eye ball and grooves in his forehead where the pellet scraped across his head. The operation was to take the pellet out of his eye. We walked up to him and just started talking about how we were both excited because this was the first time that we would get to witness an operation first hand. This guy shot up from that stretcher like he had been shot out of a cannon and his head started to swivel around. He said over and over again, "Where's my doctor? Where's my doctor?" Apparently he thought my partner and I were doctors because we had our uniforms covered and when we mentioned that this was our first operation, the guy went crazy. We just let the guy believe that we were the doctors for a while until the real doctor arrived. We went into the operating room and the suspect was anesthetized and the operation started. I was stunned to see what the doctor did next. With a suture needle he hooked the guy's eye lid into his forehead. I thought that I had seen everything up until now, but that was cold hearted. He then proceeded to

112

remove the pellet. It only took a short time, but while he was under, he stopped breathing so they had to revive him several times. Eventually, it was over and he came out of it all in relatively good shape. That was my very first operation in a hospital.

I know that there are things we see and go through that very few people except soldiers in combat ever see up close and personal. To relieve the pressure sometimes we joke about things that might seem inappropriate to others. It's our way of coping with the cruelty of this world. I tell people that it's the mental stress that can be more dangerous than the physical dangers.

Near Miss on I-71

During our time in S.W.A.T. we typically rode to work with other members living in the same area. My partner Ed and I lived relatively close together, about 30 miles from the city, and rode together a lot.

One night around 2:00 A.M we were driving home with two other members of the unit. There were four of us in the car traveling about 70 M.P.H. south on Interstate Highway 71. This stretch of the highway had three lanes going in both directions.

As we arrived in Brooklyn, a suburb, we realized we were in approximately the same location of a fatality where two of our Impact Task Force members along with a wife and a girlfriend were killed. The driver lost control and slid into a steel hauler parked on the side of the road.

There weren't too many cars on the highway this time of night. We were in the center lane, riding along discussing the day's events, when in a blink of an eye a car passed us on our left traveling about the same speed in the opposite direction. We were all speechless. Here was a car on the wrong side of the freeway going about 70 M.P.H. If the car had been one lane over, we would have hit head on. It would have been like hitting a brick wall at over 140 M.P.H. Another lucky break? Hard to believe we survived.

I had personally witnessed the results of a head on crash on the freeway. I remember when I was about 16 or 17 years old my friend and I were driving around doing much of nothing. As we were driving parallel to the freeway, we saw all kinds of rescue vehicles and all the traffic stopped. We were curious. We stopped and parked on top of the hill and ran down to see what was going on. When we got to the bottom up close to the accident scene, I saw a sight that would haunt me for a long time. There was a limbless torso unclothed except for under shorts. His head was smashed opened and his brains were all over the highway. It's something that a teenage boy or for that matter anyone doesn't need to see. In that instance the driver of the car was intoxicated, got on the highway on the wrong side and collided with a semi-tractor trailer head-on.

After the close call with the car on the wrong side, all of the images of what I had seen when I was a kid went through my head again as I thought about what could have happened.

Tracheotomy

In February, 1988, I had been working the second shift in S.W.A.T. and we had gone on several drug raids that night.

I got home around 12:30 A.M. and sat down to watch a little TV to unwind. I was feeling good except that try as I might I could not swallow which might sound strange, but I was starting to get concerned. I was spitting into the sink because nothing would go down my throat. After a short time I was getting really concerned, so I woke up my wife and told her I thought I needed to go to the hospital.

Anyone awakened to such news in the middle of the night can appreciate how unpleasant and frightening an experience this was.

When we got to the hospital, I explained my problem to the doctor. He checked my throat and then took some x-rays. When he came back in, I could see the concerned look on his face. He explained that my throat had closed up to just a hairs width and that he was going to call in a specialist. I had no problem breathing and was feeling pretty good except for the swallowing problem. After an hour or so another doctor arrived, checked my throat and gave me a quick physical. Afterwards he explained that they were going to try to put a tube down my throat to open it up. First he was going to have to put me under to perform the procedure. I asked how uncomfortable it was having the tube down my throat. He said that it's not fun but was necessary.

So the next thing I know I'm lying on the operating table getting ready to have this "procedure" done. Just before he started to put the mask over my face, I had a wave of panic. I tried to sit up. The mask was already covering my nose and mouth, and I was out for the count.

According to my wife I went into the operating room at around 3:00 A.M. and I was on the table for three hours. She was really starting to worry thinking that I had died on the table. About 6:00 A.M. it was over and they wheeled me into the intensive care unit of the hospital. I woke up a little while later. The first thing that I saw was the nurses' station and the on duty nurse sitting at her desk. I started to come around and to realize where I was. I had needles coming out of both arms, an oxygen mask covering a metal tube coming out of my throat. I realized that apparently the opening was too small to get a tube down, and they had to give me a tracheotomy. I could not believe what had happened. Just a few hours earlier I was in great shape feeling fine. Now here I was lying in this hospital bed feeling like death warmed over. When my wife came in, I realized that I couldn't talk either because the tube in my neck was spreading the vocal cords apart making speech impossible.

I spent a total of five days in the hospital while the doctors tried unsuccessfully to figure out what caused the swelling in my throat. After the five days the swelling went down and I was released from the hospital with no explanation. The worst part of the entire stay was every couple of hours they would have to come in to clean out my lungs because there were no filtering systems in play with the air going straight into my lungs. To do this was quite a trick. They had a little vacuum that they pushed down the hole in my neck and cleaned out my lungs with a violent expulsion of air.

The day before I was discharged they came into my room and the nurse came up to me and said, "You might want to hold my hand." I couldn't figure out why until the doctor approached with a long black cord with a scope on the end. Without hesitation he shoved this thing up my nose all the way down to my lungs.

After a couple of minutes he yanked it out in one quick swoop. I almost went through the roof from the pain, and I think I almost broke the nurse's hand I squeezed so hard.

They put a butterfly band-aid over the opening in my throat and sent me home. The incision healed in just a matter of days, and I went back to work a week later.

CHAPTER 8

SERGEANT

1988 – 1999

Sergeant Test

In 1988 I had been on the job going on 19 years and had been in the S.W.A.T. Unit for almost 9 years. I was happy with my job and loved being in S.W.A.T., but I started to think about retirement. I never really wanted to be a supervisor, but I could retire after 25 years and make more money as a sergeant. Plus I was watching all of the young people being promoted after only a couple of years on the job and I figured that if I waited too much longer there wouldn't be any openings left. This was the time of Affirmative Action when the government told the city that they had to hire an equal number of minorities to reflect the population of the city. If we had 40 percent minority, the city had to promote that many. It didn't matter they would have to pass over a number of whites to get to the first black. Instead of taking the most qualified they were dictated by the Federal Government's numbers. That was another reason I had to take the test at this time. I figured I could do a better job than some of my current supervisors.

There were several promotional schools in the area given by high ranking police officers. It was a good chunk of money, but I figured that if I was going to do this, I was going to go all of the way. Plus paying all of this money would give me an extra incentive and motivation.

Since the test would be given in three months, I signed up for the school in order to have time to study. Class met three times a week two to three hours a day. At the time, I worked a full time job plus several part-time jobs. I had to squeeze the school in somehow.

As time went on, I devoted more and more time to study. The philosophy of the school was if you throw enough stuff against the wall, some of it's going to stick. We would have to read a book or two and then take a four or five hundred question test. Afterward we would go over each question one at a time finding out the right answer. It was grueling and time consuming, but I continued without missing too many sessions.

Some days I would study for up to eight hours. The test was postponed for a couple of months for various reasons. I didn't want to burnout before the test. They kept postponing the test so many times that I didn't think they would ever give it. After six months it was finally scheduled. I knew the material by this time but also that over confidence was a dangerous thing. I tried to be confident but not overly confident.

Test day came, and we all gathered in the convention center downtown. Some people were so intense that to prevent them from any mishaps they would have someone follow them to make sure they got there on time. The test was about four hours long. The trick was to not make any mechanical errors and not change an answer unless you were absolutely sure. Normally the first guess is the best one.

So off we went. I read each question very slowly and thought out the answer for each one carefully. There were 100 questions on the test, but each one was very important because you could either have a job or lose one on a fraction of a point. After about an hour I was done. I looked around, but no one had gotten up to leave, so I went over each question again. Again no one had left. I felt that the test was too easy after taking hundreds of tests consisting of four to five hundred questions each.

After going over the test one more time, I said the heck with it and got up and walked out. There were several others that were leaving, but the majority was still there. I thought that I had either done really well or really bad because I had finished so quickly. There were probably 400 people taking the test in the room that I was in. It was divided into different groups of people: the patrol officers in one room, the sergeants in another and so forth. After the test we all met back at the Justice Center to talk over the different questions and what we thought the right answers were. That didn't help because each one had a different answer to the same question. We all would have to wait until the results came out.

It took about three months and finally the results of the test were posted. I just could not believe the score and where I stood on the list. I was listed number 16 out of a possible 400 that took the test. I just couldn't believe it. I was so thrilled that all of the hard work and hours that I put into this thing finally paid off. The actual test still felt like a quiz because it had been so easy.

I was promoted in September of 1988. The only problem was that at the time you couldn't stay in the same unit that you were in before being promoted. As a result I got promoted out of a good job.

When I was promoted to sergeant, we were required to leave the unit or district for another assignment. This was to prevent a person from becoming a supervisor over those he had worked with. I was assigned to the Fifth District.

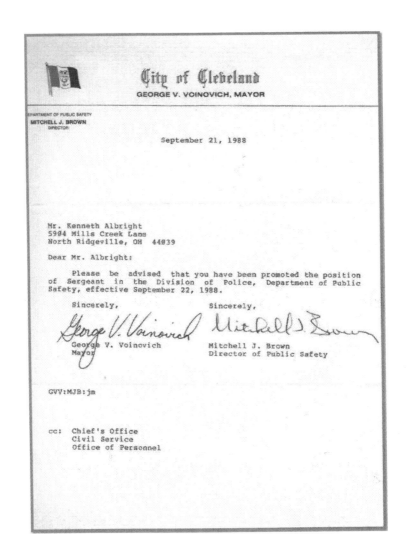

City of Cleveland
GEORGE V. VOINOVICH, MAYOR

DEPARTMENT OF PUBLIC SAFETY
MITCHELL J. BROWN
DIRECTOR

September 21, 1988

Mr. Kenneth Albright
5904 Mills Creek Lane
North Ridgeville, OH 44039

Dear Mr. Albright:

Please be advised that you have been promoted the position of Sergeant in the Division of Police, Department of Public Safety, effective September 22, 1988.

Sincerely,   Sincerely,

George V. Voinovich   Mitchell J. Brown
Mayor   Director of Public Safety

GVV:MJB:jm

cc: Chief's Office
    Civil Service
    Office of Personnel

During the 15 years that I spent in various units from 1973 to 1988 in the Task Force, Tactical Unit and the S.W.A.T. I figured that I probably kicked in anywhere from 2000 to 2500 doors on high risk searches including those of armed and dangerous suspects to your everyday local street level drug dealer.

123

Whenever the Homicide Unit was looking for a suspect and they needed a place searched, we would make an entry and secure the premises for the detectives. Any other unit that needed a place searched but felt there was a potential for trouble would call S.W.A.T. In S.W.A.T. we joked around that, "When the citizens were in trouble, they would call the police and when the police were in trouble they would call S.W.A.T."

Toward the end of my career in S.W.A.T. we were going on five or six narcotic searches a week, sometimes more. For me it got to be boring and routine which could be dangerous because when you let your guard down, it's a recipe for disaster. After a while we were hoping for something "good" to happen like a shootout or a hostage situation. That might sound crazy to the average person, but I guess you have to be a little crazy to do the job that we were doing.

CHAPTER 9

New Street Supervisor
1988 - 1989

Getting My Feet Wet

We were over in an area of the city where they were going to knock down a number of buildings to make room for the new baseball stadium that was planned for the Cleveland Indians. There was a vacant seven story high building that we were using to practice entries in a hostage situation. My job was to rappel from the roof with another member of the rappelling team and come in from the outside. We slid down the ropes, one on the right and the other on the left side of the window. We knocked out the window. As the first officer swung in, I guarded him. Then he would guard the inside as I swung in. I was hanging from the roof when one of the supervisors called up to me and asked what I was doing hanging off a roof when I was ordered to City Hall the next day to get promoted. That's how I found out about the promotional ceremony.

I was a newly promoted sergeant assigned to the Fifth District. I had been away from the mainstream of the police department for about nine years assigned to the S.W.A.T. for that time. So I was still in culture shock working the district again. I'm not suggesting S.W.A.T. was better than the district personnel, but we had to maintain a certain physical standard and weapons proficiency, so our standards were higher than those of the average district officers. During the past nine years hiring standards had also dropped considerably due to the Federal Government's policy on hiring minorities. To meet these standards they had dropped all qualifications including the entrance test and background checks. When you do that you get what they wanted: officers that reflect society as a whole, included drug dealers, thieves and any other criminals you can think of. "Affirmative action" eliminated a lot of good people. So this is what I came back to. What a surprise. Plus I had to work all three shifts again, so getting promoted maybe wasn't such a good idea.

One Sunday I was working the afternoon shift when I got a call from one of my men that he wanted to meet with me. Normally such meetings had to do with some personnel problem. Upon meeting with him, he informed me that he had just received information on the location of a suspect wanted for shooting at the police. This would be something bigger than the usual assignment a zone car would handle. As this guy had the potential of shooting it out with the police, I called for two other cars to assist.

After briefing all of the people and giving them their assignments we headed to the location. One crew went to the back and another stayed out front. Two other officers came with me to the front of the house. After we knocked and identified ourselves, the suspect's uncle opened the front door. We asked if his nephew was at home, and he informed us that he was in his bedroom. We entered the house which contained about a half dozen people. When we got inside, the suspect suddenly bolted out of a room and toward the back of the house to the rear bedroom. The officer on my left was carrying a 12 gauge shot gun. When he saw the suspect running, he shot toward the suspect striking the door frame. I think everyone was in shock including the officer that fired. I ran out the back to notify the men in the rear that everyone was okay and stay put.

Now I had to try to talk this guy from the back room which was made more difficult by the fact that we had just tried to kill him. We negotiated with him for a couple of hours. I told radio to send the S.W.A.T. so that I could release the zone cars for other assignments. One of the veteran officers took over negotiations, and after another half hour or so, he was able to persuade the suspect out. The suspect was placed under arrest, and I called off S.W.A.T. I got to experience what it was like on the other side but I still missed S.W.A.T.

As a street supervisor I would change shifts the first of every month. I was spoiled after spending nine years in S.W.A.T. and working only days and afternoons. I was still getting used to working a district again let alone as a supervisor. One of the other newly appointed supervisors that worked his whole career in a district said later on that I seemed like a fish out of water. I looked like a lost puppy. But I don't know that I did such a bad job. I did everything I needed to do to the get the job accomplished. One thing about working a district as a boss is that you get very familiar with filling out the various reports required.

I was still learning the job and making the transition from S.W.A.T. to working in a district. I had to hold roll call, assign different personnel to the zone cars and go to crime scenes to make a decision on which crime to call. In addition, I worked in the district station itself as the O.I.C. (Officer-in-Charge). There I was responsible for everything that happened from the plumbing to the welfare of the prisoners. This was a huge responsibility for a brand-new sergeant. Thankfully, there were several efficient office workers that helped out this lost soul.

Damage to My New Camaro

In 1988 I bought a brand new burgundy Chevy Camaro. It came with a V-8 engine, tinted removable T-tops and five-speed transmission. I felt great driving that car because it had the power and looks of a race car. I'm into speed and by now I was an adrenaline junkie. After getting off work about 11:00 P.M. one spring night, I was driving through the heart of the inner city on my way home. I got onto the Inner-Belt Freeway, which connected all of the interstate highways together. I was driving about 60 to 65 M.P.H. The Inner-Belt goes under several bridges through the downtown area. It's almost like going through a tunnel. As I passed under one of these bridges, the front end of the car exploded. I was in shock because I had no idea what just happened. I almost lost control of the car and immediately headed for the side of the roadway. I noticed that the front end of the car was damaged and the hood was buckled. When I finally realized what had happened, I was so angry, scared and

128

relieved all at the same time that I probably would have shot someone if I had found the culprit.

Someone on the bridge had dumped cinder blocks on to the front end of the car. The damage was so great there is no doubt in my mind that if they had hit a fraction of a second later the blocks would have come through the windshield. I could have been seriously injured or killed. The same thing has happened in the past with fatal results. After stopping on the side of the road I went around and came back to the spot under the bridge and found the bricks. Apparently, they had gotten a large box and put the bricks inside and tipped the box over sending the bricks down on top of my car. Once again I was spared. Luck? The damage was so extensive that it required a complete new front end.

That poor car of mine was so good looking that all the thieves wanted it. I had it almost stolen twice. Both times were when I was working part time at one of my jobs. Both times the ignition system was damaged making it impossible to drive without a tow. The geniuses that tried to steal it failed to realize that you had to depress the clutch to activate the switch to start the car. Each time they could have gotten the car if they had only pushed down on the clutch.

CHAPTER 10

AVIATION UNIT

1993 – 1997

Our Crew at Burke Lakefront Airport 1995

A New Opportunity

I was assigned to the Fifth District from the time I was promoted in September of 1988 to 1989. One day, I received a call from Lt. Vargo asking if I would be interested in helping him start up a new unit. When he mentioned what it was I thought that I had died and gone to heaven. The city wanted to start an Aviation Unit consisting of two supervisors and four patrol officers.

The city was looking for officers that were already licensed pilots to train to fly helicopters. Fortunately, I had my license and I was now a sergeant so I was one of only a few that qualified. I always said that the definition of success is "preparation and opportunity," and that's just what happened in this case.

When I was 12 or 13 years old, I would save my money from my paper route and go to the Lost Nation Airport (LNN) and pay a pilot to take me up for a ride. After the first time I was hooked. Needless to say, this potential position was like a dream come true.

Prelude to Flying

Back in my S.W.A.T. days I had worked with a guy at our local airport who did a lot of sky diving. At the time he probably had over 80 free falls. This was something that I had always wanted to try. I admit it was mostly a macho thing just to see if I had the courage to actually jump out of an airplane. Little did I realize that I almost bit off more than I could chew.

Oberlin (AOS) was a remote airport if you could call it an airport. It was really just an open field with a dirt runway about 1500 feet to 2000 feet long. I was always in love with flying so I could kill two birds with one stone. Fly in an airplane and jump out of one, too. This was in 1979 when we had just started the S.W.A.T. Unit and before I started my flying lessons. Actually this experience is what made me decide to fly them instead of jump out of them.

We got out to the airport bright and early. It took about four hours of training to teach me and a couple of other guys what to do and when to do it. Also we learned how to fall when we hit the ground. After the training we loaded up in a Cessna with no seats except for the pilots. The four experienced jumpers got in first because they would be leaving the plane last. Because I would be the first to jump, I was the last to enter.

The runway was short, and we had a full load so to compensate we had just enough gas to get us to altitude and back to the airport. We took off down the runway which to me seemed like forever knowing how short this field was. Finally we lifted off with nothing to spare. We skimmed the tree tops at the far end.

We started to climb. I was to jump at 3000 feet and the rest of the guys were going up to 10,000 feet so that they could free fall for about 60 seconds. I would be attached to the plane and when I jumped, the line would pull the chute open automatically. That sounded good to me. After a few minutes we finally reached our altitude of 3000 feet. I was a little nervous on the way up, but when the side door swung open and I heard and felt the noise and wind, I went from being nervous to pure fear. When I looked out and saw nothing but 3000 feet of air between me and the ground that did it. I never had been this scared in my whole life. In fact up until this point in comparison, I'd never been scared.

When it was time to leave the plane, I was to swing my legs out first and grab the struts with my left hand and the door frame with my right. When the instructor said to go, I was to jump. So I got into position. In the meantime my "buddy" was sitting in the back of the plane with this big old grin on his face. I was thinking that there was no way I could show my face the next day if I didn't jump. I figured I'm going to die so let's get it over with, and I jumped.

Now during training they tell you all about how if you're main chute won't open to cut it away and deploy your reserve chute. Let me tell you, after leaving the plane I couldn't tell you if I was right side up or upside down or which way to the earth. I think when someone gets so scared their brain actually shuts down. That's apparently what happened to me anyway.

The next conscious thought I had was when the chute opened up and I felt a tug on my shoulders. When I looked up, I saw what I thought was the chute closing up on me. I found out later that that's normal. Finally, I was floating down toward the ground. I held the two risers which controlled the steering. At this point the ride was great! It was quiet, and I was just ever so gently flowing down. Now I was being told from the ground to make sure that I turned into the wind.

The parachute has a 10 M.P.H. forward speed. If there is a 10 M.P.H. wind and you don't turn into the wind you are covering the ground at 20 M.P.H. which I found out later is not what you want to do. It HURTS!

My landing worked out just like they said it would. Now I could say that I did it, but I figured that it has to get easier with each jump. The plan was to make five static line jumps and then a "hop and pop" which meant jumping without a line attached. I would jump and pull the rip cord myself.

With each successive jump you have to pull a cord attached to your harness simulating your own cord. After five good jumps they allow you to make your first none static line jump. The progression is with each jump you wait a little longer before pulling the cord. That's the plan!

I continued jumping for several more weeks. Lo and behold it never got any easier. In fact each time was just as bad as the first if not worse because now I knew what to expect. But I was determined to stick it out. After the third jump I was about to change my mind. When I left the plane, my chute opened up like it was supposed to, but the lines were wrapped around each other which is called a "barber pole." So here I was coming down with no steering control. I had to unwrap the lines so that I wouldn't crash into anything. This was accomplished by grabbing each side and spreading them apart. This started me spinning as the lines untangled. By the time I was in control, I had drifted quite far away from the drop zone and all that I was thinking about was to get to the drop zone before I hit the ground. I was still quite a ways away when I slammed into the ground traveling about 20 M.P.H. I had forgotten to turn into the wind before landing. When I hit, I thought that I had broken something because of the pain, but there was no way that I was going to show that I was hurt. I gathered up the chute and limped back to the airport.

I made one more jump after that and then gave up sky diving for a safer hobby like flying. If someone says that they aren't scared when they jump, they are either morons or they don't realize they can die. I've heard young girls say, "That wasn't so bad; it wasn't that scary."

Early Aviation Experience

I started my flight training in early 1980 at a small airport in Strongsville, Ohio. The airport no longer exists because of progress. There's a sub-division there now, but back then it had two 2800 foot runways, one going east and west and the other one going north and south.

Flying unlike skydiving was something I had wanted to do all my life. I started training with a vengeance. I would try and get out there at least twice a week. This was at a time in my life that I was working a full time job, several part time jobs and raising a family of three growing boys.

After seven hours of training I took my first solo flight. There's no way to describe the sensation unless you have experienced it for yourself. After the first solo flight the instructor cuts the back of your shirt and hangs it up on the board, a tradition going way back. After about three months with 45 hours under my belt I took my flight test and passed with flying colors.

Over the next several years I rented planes and went flying all over the area, sometimes making longer cross country trips.

Piper Tomahawk – 1980 Beginning of my Aviation Career

I'd built up about 300 hours when I got an offer to fly for a radio station giving traffic reports on rush-hour condition both in the morning and afternoon. I jumped at the opportunity. There was no pay involved, but I got to fly for free. What more could a new pilot ask for?

I flew for this company for about six months building another 200 hours of flight time for free. Up until then I had 300 hours over an eight year period. Now 200 hours in just six months. What a deal! One little hitch in this deal was if the weather conditions were bad and we couldn't fly, we had to drive different locations giving traffic reports. Thankfully, this didn't happen too often. You have to take the good with the bad.

Training for Helicopters

We were transferred in late August and met in our office at Burke Lakefront Airport. Another dream come true: I got to leave the district which I hated and start actually being paid to do what I loved to do. What more can you ask for.

The plan was for us to receive a 12 year old Cessna 172 donated from the Ohio State Patrol and two new Schweitzer Helicopters some time the first of the year. We had to pick a flight school that trained helicopter pilots first. We had a choice of two schools in the country. One was Vero Beach Florida; the other was the University of North Dakota in Grand Forks. Was there really a choice?

Our unit was comprised of the lieutenant, myself as sergeant and four patrolmen. Our lieutenant believed in the Chain-of-Command and as second in that chain anything and everything that went wrong in the unit was my responsibility. That included all of the patrolmen and any of the problems that they got into. I never did figure out what the lieutenant's responsibility was except for taking bows at air shows and looking pretty in his tailored flight suit. Sounds like sour apples? You're right! For the first three years I took so much grief from that man that I was on the verge of quitting and that was a big decision considering how much I loved flying. Every morning I would come in and find something on my desk about something that one of the guys didn't do, some report that wasn't done; always something negative. Fortunately, he retired in September of 1993 and I was the O.I.C. for the rest of the time there.

The lieutenant decided that our rotor craft training should be done in North Dakota because that way we wouldn't be distracted. In early September of 1989 we flew to Grand Forks to start our training at the university. We would stay at a hotel a few miles from the airport and be shuttled back and forth. Our days consisted of leaving the hotel at 7:30 A.M., spending the entire day at the airport, and studying for a few more hours in the evening. After a couple of weeks the training was extended to include Saturday's.

The first day we all went out to get our first taste of what was to come. We watched a helicopter hovering around and were told we would be doing that in about a week. Hah! Let me tell you if you can pat your head, rub your stomach and jump up and down on one foot, you have a good idea of how to hover a helicopter. After a week of training we were hovering kind of by ourselves. I had to give my instructor a lot of credit. I would have the helicopter totally out of control spinning wildly in one direction and then the other all the while going up and down. I would glance over to check out whether or not he was going to take control, and I was stunned. He was just sitting there with his arms folded. You have to know the extent of your ability to know how far to let the student go before taking control.

Overview of the Operation of a Helicopter

Our Flight Line of new Schweitzer helicopters

    The collective control on the pilot's side is pulled up and down to control the pitch of the rotor blades which control the power. At the end of the collective control is the throttle control similar to a motorcycle's throttle. As you pull in the pitch, you must simultaneously add more power to maintain a constant engine RPM. We're just getting started. The cyclic control in front of you between your legs controls the movement of the helicopter forward, backward and sideways. The pedals control the tail rotors. As you pull up on the collective and add more power from the throttle, you also have to press down on one pedal to prevent the helicopter from spinning in one direction. When you move one control, you have to readjust the others to maintain control. Other than that it's a piece of cake.

As we progressed, I got to the point where I actually started to hover myself, but only with my instructor's help. I could hold it steady but if there was any movement, I would totally lose control.

We were scheduled to be there for six weeks. We were to complete a whole semester course in half the time. After a couple of weeks of training we had to complete our cross county flight which consisted of flying a three legged course. Each leg was over 100 miles long. The problem with flying over North Dakota was there were no land marks to use for navigation. That state is so flat that it is was virtually imposable to know where you are during the flight. There were a few trees around homes and buildings, but that was it. Fortunately I completed the flight without getting lost.

We stayed on this routine the entire time there: studying, flying and studying some more. Plus each morning while waiting for the ride we would have our donuts. After six weeks of eating donuts every morning and not exercising, I developed a pot belly. I was in shock because I always had a flat stomach.

Receiving my Wings from the City Council President and Chief of Police

After six weeks we all completed our training and passed our flight and written test! We were certified helicopter pilots. The plan was to hire some flight instructors after we got back to Cleveland to fly on patrol with us for the first 100 hours so that we could safely build our experience. When we got back and received our helicopters, we made arrangements to drive down to Columbus, Ohio, and fly with their Aviation Unit to get a little training before we started ours. They had been in business for a dozen years or so at this point and were pretty proficient. We rode along with them for about a week and learned a lot.

We started flight patrol flights early in 1990 with two brand new Schweitzer Helicopters. A few years later we got another one for a total of three helicopters. We also got one

Cessna 172 for our fixed wing aircraft. We were a full-fledged Aviation Unit now.

The helicopters were used mostly for patrolling the city and the plane for traffic enforcement or aerial surveillance of suspects in a crime. Once a week we would get together with the Traffic Unit and arrange to meet at a certain location in the city that had measured lines on the side of the interstate. Using the lines we could time motorists clocking their speed. This was done with a stop watch. After timing them we would radio to the motorcycles and give a brief description of the car, the speed and the lane the car was in. After the speeder was stopped, we both would log the stops. We would orbit the area for about two hours with an average of 40 to 60 traffic stops. Normally, we would have a spotter in the back of the plane to help out, but every now and again I would have to do it all myself.

Commendation

Mission over the City of Cleveland

In December of 1991 we were patrolling in the area of the Fourth District. We heard over the radio that a Dairy Mart Store had been robbed and were given a general description of the suspect. In the helicopter we could cover the entire city in just a matter of minutes.

We got on the scene in no time and started our search for the suspect. After 15 or 20 minutes one of the zone cars in the area stopped a suspect fitting the description. While they were questioning him, the suspect struck the officer and fled down Warner Road into a ravine surrounded by woods. It would be nearly impossible to locate a person at night in that remote area.

Within a short time the entire area was surrounded with police cars covering all of the possible ways that the suspect might try to escape. The problem I had was that I had to stay a lot higher than I wanted because of high tension wires surrounding the ravine.

I'm always up for pushing the envelope, so I decided that the only way to spot the suspect in the thick woods was to get low. Down I went skimming the tree tops. Due to the location of the towers I had to make tight turns to avoid the wires. It was around midnight and pretty dark, so I really had to be aware of where I was to keep from running into anything. My observer would have to do most of the spotting while I flew the aircraft.

As we got lower, my observer spotted something that might be a person lying on the ground. As we slowed and shone our light we could identify the suspect and saw that he had a gun still in his out stretched hand. The challenge now was to direct the officers on the ground to the suspect. As we continued broadcasting the location, we could see the officers all around him almost tripping over him unable to see him in the dark woods. Finally, they located him and placed him under arrest. It was a big relief that the dangerous, armed suspect was arrested without anyone being hurt. I would just hate to think what could have happened if we had not been in the area and able to help out. Without help from the helicopter, officers on the ground would be in grave danger because of the terrain and darkness. That's in my opinion what the Aviation Unit is all about.

The unit is also invaluable during high speed chases. Ground vehicles can back off a short ways while we stay with the suspect vehicle. This way the suspect has a tendency to slow down since he feels that he is no longer being chased. Even if the suspect bails and is on foot, there is no way that he is going to lose us in the air. I've had several suspects actually give themselves up to us because they realized they couldn't lose us. They would just sit down with their hands up. We would then call for a zone car to come and pick them up.

I did not feel especially worthy of the award I was subsequently presented for my part in the capture of the suspect.   Police   departments,   however,   look   for opportunities to present awards, so I accepted mine politely fully aware that we had just done our job that night and thankful everyone went home safe.

Aerobatics

After flying for two or three thousand hours I became quite comfortable, sometimes even bored just flying around. I'm the kind of guy that likes to push the envelope, or in other words do something exciting to get the juices flowing.

During the early part of the year we would be requested to fly to different city schools to talk to the kids about various jobs available out in the working world. People from all walks of life would participate in these career days.

From April until the end of May we flew into about 20 to 25 schools.   Members of the police mounted unit would attend with their horses. Policeman from the S.W.A.T. unit, the bicycle unit plus fireman were there. Also attending were people who worked in the private sector.

One day I met a local church group in the Metro parks and gave them a demonstration of the helicopter. I normally don't do this but on this day there was enough open space with no obstacles in the area. The field was about 300 yards long and about 100 yards wide and was raised up above the rest of the area. It was a great practice area.

As I flew over the area at altitude 500 feet AGL, I saw the group at one end of the field. I thought that I would sneak up on them by dropping down below the trees and fly just above the river following it to the field. Then just as I got to the field, I would pop up over the trees and fly across the field as fast as I could go which was about 100 M.P.H. As I got to the group, I would pull back on the cyclic and go straight up. As I lost most of my airspeed, I would kick the left pedal spinning the helicopter's nose down and pick up speed as I approached the ground. Just before hitting the ground I would level out going in the opposite direction at full speed. This maneuver is called return to target which was something that the military pilots used in Vietnam. I would then do a quick stop and do a little show before shutting down. This is not taught in flight school but something that I read about. I tried it and it worked great.

Another thing I would like to do would be to fly over Edgewater Park by Lake Erie and fly just a few feet above the tree tops at full speed so close that I would have to pop up a little to miss some higher trees. When I got to the end of the park, I would roll the helicopter over on its side and drop below the cliffs pulling out just above the water. Great fun!

There were a few times that being proficient in flying helped out when there was something happening that was out of the norm. One time in the winter I was coming in to the airport for a landing and when I got about 40 to 50 feet above the runway the entire inside of the glass fogged up so that I was completely blind. This is called an "inversion." The air temperature is warmer on the surface and colder above the surface. There I was in the air maybe 50 feet above the ground and I had no idea of up or down. The helicopter that we were flying wasn't equipped to fly in zero visibility or IFR conditions. The only thing that I could do was to continue down without changing my rate of descent and hope that I didn't hit the ground too hard. Fortunately I made it safely to the ground. The helicopter is like a big glass greenhouse. So when it fogged up, the entire cockpit fogged up.

Another time during the summer we were on night patrol over the city. There had been showers in the area all day, nothing serious. As the night went on, the weather started to get pretty bad so we started to ease our way toward the airport. We got an urgent call from the control tower at the airport reporting a major thunderstorm approaching from the west. I kicked it in gear and started high tailing it back to the airport before the storm hit. When I was still several miles away, I could see the storm barreling down on us at a high rate of speed.

Here we were in a high speed chase with a large thunder storm. I figured that if I didn't get back before the storm hit, I would have to put down in a parking lot until the storm passed, and I didn't really want to do that. On we went getting closer and closer to the airport. I could see that it was going to be very close. About a mile away the storm came over the airport covering it like a blanket. Just as it reached the end of the runway, I was coming in fast toward the ground. By the time I reached the ground, I could only see just a few feet in front of the helicopter. The

Tower called requesting my location as they could not see us and were hoping we were down. I confirmed our location, hovered back to the hanger, landed, and shut down.

To keep from getting bored I would fly through downtown Cleveland lower than the buildings and zig zag around them like a maze. This might freak out a novice flyer. Also in the warmer months we would fly without the doors on because with all that glass the cockpit would heat up like a greenhouse. Someone that had never flown without doors (which would be most everyone) during a tight right-hand turn would look out the door at the ground and just about be on my lap trying not to fall out. This was usually about 500 feet to 1000 feet above the ground.

Helicopters are totally different in the way they fly. An airplane needs the air rushing over its wings to stay aloft where a helicopters spinning rotor blades keeps it in the air. In a helicopter we can stop moving and come to a hover. To move forward you need to drop the nose so that the rotor blade will start pulling the aircraft through the air. To accomplish this you just drop the nose and off you go. I would show my passenger how we can be completely stopped and in a matter of five or six seconds be going close to 100 m.p.h. I would come to an out-of-ground hover and zero out the airspeed indicator so that we are in a hover. Then I would nose the aircraft over so that we were looking straight down. Instead of dropping as it appeared, we were actually picking up speed. It's a great experience.

Engine Problems Over Edgewater Park

One night while flying routine patrol we were on the far west side of Cleveland near Cleveland Hopkins International Airport, (CLE). When that close to a busy airport you are required by law to maintain contact with the airport. So as the pilot I was monitoring three different radios at the same time. That might sound hard which it is initially, but like anything else with a little experience, it became routine.

I had a fairly new observer with me. This was a volunteer position with the Aviation Unit lasting three months at a time. The problem with that system was sometimes we would get people that were totally unable to handle the job. Other times we would get people that were really good and did a great job, but then we would lose them after three months.

The job description was to handle the police radios, to locate addresses on the map, and to relay that information to the pilot. The observer also made the daily duty reports logging all of the activities and radio assignments of the day. Sounds fairly easy but you have to remember when we are flying high over the city the perspective is totally different than on the ground. It takes a while to get your bearings.

We did most of our patrols at night during the high crime times, so we got pretty proficient at locating different areas of the city quickly. After a while I got to know the city so well that it resembled a lit up road map at night. I could, nine times out of ten, find the street without the use of the map and within a couple of houses from the address given. That's called experience!

We had just finished checking out a break-in, finding nothing, we cleared the area. This was our last assignment of the night and we headed back toward the airport around 1:30 A.M.

We were still over the First District which is mostly residential when the helicopter started to shake violently. This got my attention because I had never experienced anything like this. Immediately, I started going through all the possible causes. My initial thought was that I had hit something knocking the main rotor blades out of balance. I eased back on the power thinking that without the load on the blades the vibration would subside a little which it did not. At this point I thought that it might be the engine getting ready to freeze up. If that happened, I would have to go into an autorotation. The possibilities of coming down over a residential area without anyone getting hurt were remote. So I wasn't all that excited about that happening.

I weighed the options and decided to try to make it back to the airport which was still about 10 miles away. I informed my observer of what I was going to do and told him to keep an eye open for any parking lot or open area so that if the engine quit I would have some safe place to land. At the time it wasn't funny, but thinking about it after everything was all over I realized how nervous he was. He would shout out every couple of seconds, "There's a lot on the right. There's another one on the left." This went on until we got over a large park by the lake where I could land without any problems. We called dispatch and informed them of our intentions. After landing and shutting down the engine, I restarted it to determine whether the problem involved blades or the engine itself. As soon as I restarted the engine, the vibration started. That took care of that question.

It was about 1:45 A.M. now and we could not just leave the helicopter sitting on the sand, so initially I thought about getting a district zone car to sit on it until morning when we could bring out a mechanic. There were no cars available so plan "B" was to call for a tow truck with a flat bed and have two marked patrol cars escort it back downtown to the airport. So that's what I did. The tow truck drove extremely slowly down the freeway with two marked cars with their overhead lights on flanking either side. We got back all in one piece and survived to fly another day.

After a few days they tore the engine down and discovered that two valves in the engine were blocked and that this 4 cylinder engine was operating on just two cylinders. That could cause the vibration we experienced.

When these things happen at the time you don't really think too much about it. You chalk it up to just being lucky and it wasn't your time. It wasn't my time because the Lord of the universe, Creator of all decided that it wasn't my time. I joke around about our guardian angels. The ones assigned to me are getting really worn out over the years.

Secret Service Detail for Clinton

In the Aviation Unit we were required to assist the Secret Service detail during the presidential visits to the city. I have been on these details many times before, so I knew what was expected of me. I've worked with most of the same agents over the years while I was in S.W.A.T. and a number of times since I was in the Aviation Unit. The difference was that in S.W.A.T I was a sniper and would hook up with their sniper team. We would pick a strategic location in the area of where the President was going to be and set up our post. Sometimes this wasn't too bad, but other times when the weather was bad, it could be miserable.

Our duties in the Aviation Unit were to hook up with an assigned agent, take off about 10 minutes before the motorcade started, and fly the motor route. We checked on anything that looked suspicious like a broken down vehicle or anyone in the area that looked suspicious. If we found anything we would have it checked out. The rule was that I couldn't fly over the specific route. I had to fly parallel to it which to me was so bizarre that it didn't make a bit of sense, but who am I to question the U.S. Government.

It was a mid-winter day and President Clinton was running for re-election. One of his stops was the college on the west side of town about a 20 minute drive. By air I could make it in about 10 minutes. Off I went with this young agent. I could tell by his actions and facial expressions that he wasn't too comfortable with this whole idea of flying around in this tiny little egg beater. The weather was looking a little bad, and there were snow squalls predicted in the area. I wasn't too concerned knowing the area like I did and being able to land just about anywhere if it got too bad. So off we went heading toward the college, checking the route as we went. I was flying about 500 feet above the ground because any higher it would be harder to see. We got out there with no problem and after the motorcade arrived, I found out that the President was going to be there

153

for an hour so I decided to land on the grounds and shut down.

As we waited, I could see the sky getting pretty overcast and the ceiling was dropping. I informed the agent that we might have to leave early because if it got too bad, we would be stuck here on the ground. A short while later I decided that it was time to vacate the area, because I sure didn't want to have to leave the helicopter here on a college campus. That would be just asking for trouble. I cranked up and off we went. As soon as I was airborne, I was in the clouds. Normally, this wouldn't be any problem, but as I mentioned before, in this particular aircraft we weren't equipped with the instruments to fly blind. So as I got into the clouds and couldn't see anything; I slowed the aircraft down and started to drop lower to get out of the clouds. I got down to just about the telephone pole level and could see fairly well. I couldn't get any higher, or I would be back in the soup.

There are two types of flying. One is called VFR or visual flight rules and the other one is IFR or instrument flight rules. For VFR you need to see at least three miles with a 1000 foot ceiling. For IFR you can fly on your instruments, but you have to file a flight plan. Well the rules are a little different in a helicopter than with an airplane. We can fly lower if need be, and the IFR restrictions are a little different. The type of flying I was doing at the time I like to call IFR or, "I Follow Roads." I had lived in Cleveland my whole life, so I knew the area quite well. I followed the main road north which I knew would get us to the downtown area. I had to watch out for any wires and

154

anything higher than a telephone pole. I took it very slow all the way to Brook Park Road where the ceilings were up to about 1,500 feet. As I picked up speed and altitude, the agent looked over and asked if that was normal procedure, and I assured him that it was and we were perfectly safe. Hey, I didn't want to scare the poor guy.

Assisting Officers in Trouble

While flying patrol our job was to check out locations for any criminal activity and report back to radio of the disposition. Another job was to assist the zone cars with anything that they might need. These duties were assisting in a high speed chase, or locating a suspect in back yards by lighting up the area, or just being in the area for a traffic stop. Just knowing someone was there to help in case of trouble was comforting. Sometimes we were quite frustrated though because we were limited in how much we could do from the air to help officers on the ground.

One night we heard a frantic call for help from a zone car in the Second District. They responded to a break-in at a local school and when they arrived, they observed a broken window at the back. They entered and after a search discovered the suspect hiding in one of the classrooms. They placed him under arrest, but as they were coming back to their zone car with the juvenile suspect, they were surrounded by a hostile crowd. Apparently, the juvenile lived in the neighborhood, and the crowd was attempting to take the suspect away from the officers by force. I tried to scare the neighbors away by lighting them up with the spot light, but it did not do any good.

Well let me tell you if a frantic cry from a fellow officer needing help doesn't get your blood flowing, nothing will. We started to orbit the area and light it up to help the officers without much success. They were being attacked by the neighbors, and it would take the nearest zone car several minutes to reach them. I made the decision to land at the school yard and do what I had to do to help out the officers. When we landed, I told my partner to get out and run over to give the zone car guys some help. After he got out, I went back up into a hover about three feet off the ground. The only thing that I could think of was to try to drive the crowd back away from the officers. I had seen on the Discovery Channel that in Australia they could herd cattle with helicopters, so I figured why not try that tactic.

I maneuvered into position between the officers and the crowd and started moving back and forth keeping the mob at bay. This worked until help arrived. Between the noise of the engine and the twirling rotor blades the people decided that it wasn't worth dying for.

After landing and picking up my partner, we left the area satisfied we had done a good job. Of course that wasn't authorized and the good lieutenant let me know the next day. I felt that you have to do what you have to do to protect your people.

Locating House Fires over the City

While flying patrol over the city, there were times we would look out several miles away and see smoke rising from a house fire. It would take us only a couple minutes to locate the address and call for the Fire Department. We were able to give them the exact location and cut down on their response time. We could see the smoke coming up in thick billowing black waves, and when the Fire Department started to hose it down, it would turn white. That's how we could tell they were on the scene.

One night we were flying over an industrial area of the city and saw a fire in a dumpster in the rear of a factory. This factory was enclosed by a large chain link security fence, and the fire was in a location impossible to see from the street. We called for the Fire Department to respond and stayed in the area to direct them to the fire's location. Once they found it, they were able to put it out fairly quickly. If we had not spotted the fire, it could have potentially spread to the entire neighborhood.

The Mooning

Another time while flying patrol on the West side of the city we observed a large fire in the back yard of a house. We immediately flew over the area and observed a large bonfire in the rear of the property. Several people were sitting around it on couches and chairs. It's illegal to have an open fire in the city limits, so instead of calling it in, we turned on the spot light and made several orbits letting them know to put out the fire. After several minutes of this, one of the guys got up off his couch and "mooned" us. With this, I thought, 'no more mister nice guy' and called for a zone car to arrest this male for having an open fire and indecent exposure. It wasn't long that a car pulled up in front of the house. I directed the two officers to the rear of the property and identified the male. They immediately placed hand

157

cuffs on him, walked him out to the police car and drove away. I know that I'm not supposed to feel good in someone else's misery, but boy did that feel good.

Another chase to Willoughby

We were on routine patrol one night when we heard a call on the radio of a stolen auto in the First District. We're always up for a good chase especially in the helicopter, so we headed in that direction. Fortunately, the suspect was headed in our direction. If he had gone west, we would not have been able to follow him because we would be in Cleveland Hopkins Airport air space where we would not have been allowed. So unbeknownst to this guy he probably would have been able to get away had he gone in that direction. We picked him up in the Second District going north on I-71, travelling at a high rate of speed. If it's just a traffic violation and the chase is creating a danger to the citizens the supervisor will call it off. This is what happened in this case, but I couldn't leave it alone. One benefit of our helicopter is that when the cars are called off, we can keep abreast of the situation and contact upcoming districts informing them of the location. I called the Second District and they took up the chase until he went into the Third District heading east on Route 2. As he was about to leave the city, all of the districts called off the chase, but like I said I didn't want to let it go. His reckless driving and disregard for anyone else on the roadway was causing a hazardous situation. So as he was leaving the City of Cleveland, I got on the state wide radio and started to broadcast to the suburbs. This guy was going so fast he was pulling away from me. It's a good thing that it was dark because I just kept my eyes glued on his tail light. I didn't see any other police car in the area, so I figured he was home free.

As he continued, he was so far ahead it was getting hard to see him. Then he did something I didn't expect. He got off the freeway at Route 306 and got back on coming west right towards us. If he had just kept going, he would have been long gone. He was approaching a construction area where the lanes cut down to one lane with concrete barriers blocking the other lanes. This guy was going so fast that by the time he realized there was a barrier in his way, it was too late. He hit the wall full speed, and from our view it was unbelievable. The car literally cut itself in half. The front half was from the driver's seat forward, and the back half was from the rear seat back. Both halves went spinning and I could see the head lights were still on.

When everything stopped, I could see the driver lying on the road not moving. We immediately called for life-flight from Metro Hospital and called the local police department and notified them of the location and what happened. We waited until the life-flight was approaching and then left the area to get out of their way.

1996 World Series Incident

The Cleveland Indians baseball team finally made it to the World Series after 52 years. They hadn't won since 1948. In the 1954 series with the New York Yankees they were swept by the Yankees winning the first four games. The series is the best out of seven games. We were playing the Atlanta Braves. Little did I know at the time that I would be living in the Atlanta area a few years later.

One night the Traffic Commissioner called me over the air and wanted to meet me at the airport. Now Burke Lakefront Airport is probably one of the very few airports that is in the downtown area of any major city in the country. This makes it very convenient for corporate airplanes coming to town. The problem is that it's located on the edge of Lake Erie, and in the winter with the winter winds coming across the lake from Canada it gets very cold.

I flew back to the airport where I met with the Commissioner who stated that he wanted to go up with me and fly over the downtown area checking on the traffic around the stadium. This was a night game and the third game of the series. We were ahead by two games at the time. We lifted off and flew to the stadium which is just on the south side of the city. The stadium has a capacity of 43,000. As you might imagine, it was filled to the capacity. We started to circle overhead and to show off to the Commissioner I was getting as low as possible without any danger to anyone on the ground. We were about 300 feet above the stadium traveling at only about 30 M.P.H.

Typically, when the home team hits a home run the stadium shoot off a rocket that explodes about 400 feet in the air. You guessed it, we were just about on top of the stadium when someone on the home team hit a home run. Out of the corner of my eye, I saw a rocket shoot past us missing the rear end of the helicopter by a few feet. I was so surprised that I immediately banked sharply to avoid any more fireworks. If that rocket had hit the tail rotor, we would have been in real trouble. That's what keeps the helicopter from spinning in the opposite direction of the main rotor blades at the same speed.

The Commissioner never knew how close he came to being shot out of the sky, and I sure wasn't going to tell him. After a few more minutes, we flew back to the airport and landed. The Commissioner was very pleased with the flight and that there were no traffic problems. I got out with my legs still shaking, but there was no way I was going to let on how close we came to having a big problem. I'm convinced that if that rocket had hit the helicopter it would have had done some major damage. It might not have knocked us out of the sky, but we wouldn't be doing much flying after that.

Helicopter Crash

I was flying routine patrol over the City of Cleveland. I had been doing this same job for about eight years at the time and felt really comfortable. We would fly two hours with a partner and then land for two hours, and the other partner would fly for the second two hours. I had flown the first patrol so my partner was scheduled for this flight, but I decided to take it instead. After 3000 hours of flying in different weather conditions, landing in tight spots in the city and practicing for emergencies, I became relaxed.

This night was no different than all of the others. I was flying and we were into our second hour of our second flight of the night. I was flying with the collective lever locked down (control for the power which controls the pitch of the rotor blades) and with my feet on top of the pedals "relaxed". At about 23:10 hours after receiving a radio assignment to check for prowlers, I heard a loud bang. A fraction of a second later I felt and heard the main rotor blades starting to wind down. The sound reminded me of a wounded animal dying. You hear all of the time how when you get into a life and death situation time slows down. Well take it from someone who has been there, it does. My mind seemed like it went into automatic control. I remember reacting and looking for a place to land, but it all seemed unreal. I don't remember consciously thinking about what to do. I just remember doing what I was taught in training.

The first thing that I did was drop the collective going into an autorotation, and then I checked to see if I had any power by pulling up on the collective. But each time I tried, I would lose rotor R.P.M. (revolutions per minute). I knew at that point I had no power whatsoever. The peculiar thing with a helicopter is that while in an autorotation you have to maintain 55 M.P.H. forward speed to create the slowest rate of descent which is 2000 F.P.M (feet per minute).

We were flying at about 500 feet A.G.L. (above ground level) which computes to having about 15 or 20 seconds before we were on the ground. Since my view to the left was unobstructed, that's the way I started to look for a place to set down. I remember having a conversation with my partner about where to land. What was really strange at this point was I never had any thought that we were in danger. I was so comfortable in this environment that it was no big deal. I didn't think about death or even injuries. Of course, later on I realized how much danger we had really been in. I was looking to my left and as I was looking around all that I saw were homes, business, factories and high tension wires. I still had lateral control and to my left I saw a black space between two large buildings. I hoped it was a parking lot. I banked to my left making a 180 degree turn toward the black space. As I entered between the buildings, we were lower than they were at this point in time going about 60 M.P.H.

As I approached the parking lot, I noticed that there was a chain link fence on the other side of the lot next to the street. The lot was smaller than I had hoped for but there was no turning back now.

I entered the back part of the parking lot and when I saw the fence, I quickly calculated that at this speed I would run out of parking lot and hook the skids on the fence flipping us upside down. Not good. I pulled back on the cyclic to stop the forward motion standing the helicopter on its tail. When I leveled out with zero airspeed, I was still over 50 feet in the air. We dropped out of the sky striking the ground with such force that the tail boom spilt off and the main rotor blade flexed down striking the tail boom. During that brief moment we started to roll due to the torque of the blades, but fortunately we turned 180 degrees facing the way that we came.

Ideally to do an autorotation correctly you would wait until you were about 50 feet from the ground and start slowing the aircraft by lifting the nose. As we continued slowing down, at about 10 feet leveling out I pulled the collective up just prior to touching down using the inertia of the blades to cushion the landing.

That's not the ideal way of doing an autorotation, but when you run out of real-estate you do the best you can.

When we struck the ground, I felt a twinge in the back of my neck and noticed that my partner was out of the helicopter running down the street. The first thing I thought was, "Wow he didn't even check on my condition." I shut the fuel flow, turned off the electric power, unfastened my safety belt and jumped from the wreckage forgetting to remove my headset which was attached by a plug. When I jumped out, my head snapped back ripping the plug out of the socket almost taking my head with it.

In the mean time I started to take survey of the damage and our location. I was not exactly sure where we were, so as strange as this might sound I walked out to the street and asked a passerby our location. In the meantime my partner came back and called for assistance.

We waited for what seemed like forever for help to reach us. We could hear sirens all around us but no one arrived on the scene of the accident. Come to find out later my partner gave out the wrong location giving it 10 blocks away. Eventually fire rescue arrived and conveyed us to the hospital. They thought I might have a back or neck injury, so they put me on a backboard and strapped me down. They must have hit every pot hole in the city. If I hadn't been injured to start with, I would surely have had a bad back by the time I got the hospital.

Once we got to the hospital we were greeted by a deluge of representatives from various departments of the city

164

from the Chief of Police on down. They were there either to see if we were ok, or to check on how many law suits the city was in for due to damages caused by the crash.

The next day after the dust had settled, we went back to the hanger to check on the damages in the day light and to start on a ton of reports. When I had checked the helicopter over, I discovered the collective still had the friction lever on. On a normal day it would have been extremely difficult to move the handle, but I have no memory of having any problems moving it. As a matter of fact it was fairly easy. Another peculiarity that I discovered was the pedals which are attached to steel rods about an inch thick had both had been snapped in half. I was dumbfounded! The only thing that I can figure is that I had a ton of adrenaline pouring into my system. I do remember that I started to shake when I got into the fire rescue vehicle which was a sign of the adrenaline leaving my body. I had experienced that same thing after a shooting incident a few years earlier.

Surprisingly, I had no difficulty getting back into the air. As a matter of fact I was up the very next day flying over the area of the crash trying to locate my path and the parking lot. As I think back on my brush with death, I know that God spared my life. All of my training and experience would have counted for nothing, if my Lord and Savior hadn't taken me and guided me to that specific spot to put down in. It turned out to be the only place within blocks that we could have landed and still walked away. Statistics prove that your chance of surviving a helicopter crash in the middle of a large metropolitan area is small. This was a miracle!

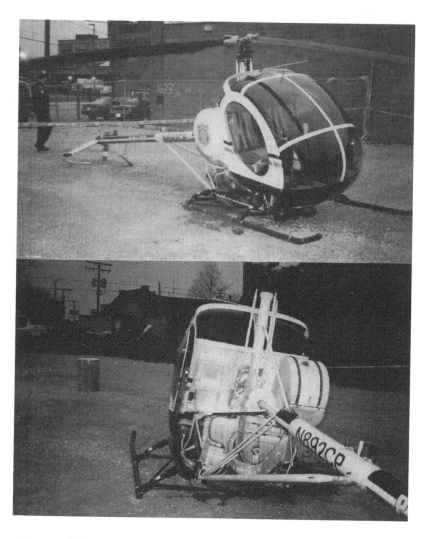

My crash-landed Helicopter 23:10 hrs. March 19th. 1997 –
Factory parking lot East 40th and Payne Avenue.

I was just happy to be alive. I was stunned with a ceremony at City Hall and to be awarded the Distinguished Service Medal.

Distinguished Service Medal

Sergeant Kenneth Albright

The Distinguished Service Medal is awarded to a Cleveland Police Officer who demonstrated a high degree of personal initiative, performs substantially above normal requirements and in an exemplary manner, or contributes significantly to the achievement of law enforcement goals.

On March 19, 1997, Sergeant Albright was piloting a Division of Police helicopter on a routine patrol flight when he heard a loud bang and discovered that his engine had stopped running. Sergeant Albright immediately initiated emergency procedures for landing the helicopter. As the helicopter fell, Sergeant Albright maneuvered it toward an open parking lot and away from residential homes. Keeping a clear head under stressful circumstances, Sergeant Albright managed to land the helicopter with only minor injuries to himself and his passenger.

Sergeant Albright's calm, instinctive reaction, high degree of personal initiative and courageous behavior, prevented a potentially disastrous situation from occurring.

For bravery of the highest order and for professionalism under the most stressful of circumstances, it is an honor to bestow upon you, Sergeant Albright the Distinguished Service Medal. Signed Mayor Michael R. White, the Director of Public Safety and the Chief of Police.

Where else can you crash a helicopter owned by the city and then turn around and receive an award. Cool!

The big question looming in a pilot's mind - what will I do in case of an emergency? When tested, will I keep a cool head and do the things that I was trained to do, or will I panic and kill myself and whoever is with me. I guess I passed the test.

It's one thing to be flying a small single engine airplane over an open area 1,000 feet above the ground and lose an engine. In that case you should have plenty of time to figure out what's wrong and fix it, or look for a place to put down safely. It's all together a different situation to lose an engine when flying over a large city at night in a helicopter. In that case you are limited on where to set down the aircraft. In a helicopter the minimum descent rate is 2,000 feet per minute and at 500 feet that comes to 15 seconds. In a small plane flying at 1,000 feet your decent rate is about 1,000 feet per mile traveled and you have at least three to five minutes. There is a huge different in the two scenarios.

As I related in my earlier story about the crash I had no thought about us getting hurt or even killed. When the engine exploded and I lost complete power, my only thought was, "Ok we have a problem. Let's work it out and figure out if I have any power or not and where am I going to land this thing." I know that the Lord was with me in it all and gave me that assurance so that I didn't panic and showed me where to land safely. I owe it all to Him.

Personnel Problems

After the Aviation Unit had been in existence for some time we began changing personnel. The lieutenant decided that one of our officers had to go because he was creating problems. This guy flew in Vietnam on several tours of duty so he was well qualified to fly, but he was a loose cannon. It was decided that he should be transferred back to his original district. As the second in command it was my job to inform him of his transfer. It's not that I couldn't handle this, but I just felt that the officer in command really should have dealt with such a serious issue. As I said before he was the poster boy for the unit and took all the glory and avoided the negative. When the time came, I pulled this individual aside and informed him of his transfer. His eyes watered. He loved being in the unit, and he was hurt. This was one of the hardest things I had to do as a supervisor, but I figured that if you take on the job of a supervisor, you take on the responsibility also.

So we put out an anticipated assignment request through the department. The qualifications were at least five years on the police department and a pilot's license. We got several applicants, but one I'll call Fred was more than qualified. He had several hundred hours flying military helicopters and was in the U.S. Army Reserve for several years. The problem was the lieutenant didn't like his personality. He thought that he was too cocky. That was like pot calling the kettle black. But after some persuasion on my part, I finally talked him into having Fred transferred.

After the lieutenant retired, I took charge of the unit. Now we were down to just five pilots and two observers that were only detailed for three months at a time. Over the next several years two more officers retired, so now I was getting desperate for new people. I was down to three officers including myself, and Fred was up for promotion. I got the word that the Traffic Commissioner wanted to transfer him to a district as is the custom for being promoted. That would leave us with two officers including myself, so few we couldn't function at more than part time.

I know that this was not proper procedure and struggled over that and trying to save my unit. I knew the lieutenant that worked for the Deputy Chief so I took the chance and went over to see the D.C. personally to plead my case. I'm sure if it was ever discovered by the Traffic Commissioner, I would have been transferred at the very least. I got the chief's assurance that Fred would stay where he was. What a relief.

Over the next year or so we finally got new people. They would be with us for a 90 day trial period. I also had Fred, who at this time had been promoted to sergeant, get his instructor's rating so that we could train the new people in-house. Otherwise we would have to send them out of town for their training which would have cost the city four times as much.

Once again I had to do the hardest thing as a supervisor and fire someone from the unit. This guy wanted to fly more than anything in the world; but after being an observer for several months, he hadn't a clue where he was over the city. One of the most important parts of being in the Aviation Unit is getting to a location quickly and knowing where you are at all times. Plus our instructor took him flying in a fixed wing airplane, our Cessna 172. This guy had a license, but when he demonstrated his flying, he nearly crashed the plane. Between that and his not being able to find his way around the city, I had to let him go before the 90 days were up.

Unfortunately, after Fred made sergeant things started to change. He was still a dedicated officer wanting to just do his job to the best of his ability, but he developed an attitude. There can be only one boss in any outfit. Here we are equal in rank. The difference was that I was the O.I.C., had been this rank for several years, and had 25 years on the job in comparison to his six months as a sergeant and five years on the police department. Things went along fine for a while and then started to change. It had gotten to the point Fred was barely talking to me. One day I cornered him and asked him just what was going on. He stated, "You know what's going on. You're trying to stab me in the back." I was taken aback and couldn't believe what he said. I tried to reason with him but he refused to listen.

Over the next couple of months things went along about the same until there was another promotional test coming up. I figured with the way things were, if Fred got promoted before me, he would make my life a living hell. We both studied hard and took the test. Finally the results came out, and they were very disappointing to say the least. Fred scored number 7, and I scored 42. Now I knew that my days as O.I.C. were numbered. Also Fred had become our instructor pilot for the unit and every two years we were required to go up with an instructor for our bi-annual flight review. I have been flying for about 15 years at this point with about 2500 hours of flight time, so I was pretty seasoned. I believe Fred had a problem with me and instead of an hour on the ground and another hour in the air, he put me through the most grueling interview that I could imagine. It took us two days just to get through the ground testing before we even got in the air. I felt like he wanted to make me feel like a failure and let me know that he was now superior to me.

When he made lieutenant, I knew my goose was cooked. I was put on the night shift to fly patrol while he was on days. I went to the Traffic Commissioner who was our boss and told him that if I wasn't transferred immediately, I was going to take an early retirement and I meant it. I saved this man's job in the Aviation Unit several times over the years, and it hurt me more than anything else for him to believe that I would do anything to hurt someone else, especially one of my co-workers.

Leaving on Patrol – Burke Lakefront Airport (BKL)

As it turned out, it was a better deal than I could have even planned for. I was transferred to the Motorcycle Unit shortly after that. I know that the Lord was still looking out for me even at a time like this when I had all those negative feelings in my heart.

CHAPTER 11

PIPES AND DRUMS

1997

In 1997 the police department started up their own Pipes and Drum Unit. It consisted of bag pipes and different types of drums and would perform at various events and in parades.

I have no musical ability at all but the sergeant starting it up wanted someone to be the drum major. This is the person in front of the parade who leads the whole thing by holding a long baton and giving directions during the parade. They wanted a tall person, and since I'm over 6 feet they asked me. I had no experience in anything what so ever like this but when I was asked, I said sure because I'm always up for trying new things.

Our uniforms included a police type blouse, a kilt with long white stockings and boots. I also needed to purchase a big black fury hat with a feather on it. Sounds weird, but actually it wasn't all that bad.

Standing in Review 'Pipes and Drums'

We practiced twice a week and after several months began to go to different events to play and march. The one that I remember the most was the Eliot Ness funeral. Eliot Ness was the Federal Agent responsible for taking down Al Capone in 1932. He and his men were known as the "Untouchables" because back then everyone could be bought from judges on down to police officers. The

Untouchables were called that because people tried to buy them off but they wouldn't take bribes. They even had a TV series about them in the late 1950's and early 1960's. Ness became the Safety Director in the City of Cleveland in the late 1930's. He was brought in to clean up the corrupted police department. During his administration he did clean up the department and actually designed the modern day traffic light system. During those years Ness was in Cleveland there were a series of murders committed by the first serial killer ever in Cleveland. The bodies were found without the heads and sometime- without limbs. The killer became known as the "torso killer". This killing spree went on for about 10 years, and there were several suspects but no evidence. Eventually the killings just stopped after a grand total of 12 murders. Eliot Ness never found the killer, his popularity diminished, and the killings went unsolved.

As the story goes, he would sit around the bar getting drunk telling war stories about his exploits back in Chicago. No one believed him at the time thinking that he was just another drunk talking big.

Eliot passed away just before the TV series started and was survived by his wife and adopted son. His body was cremated. Eventually his urn was stored in the attic of his stepson's house. After his widow died, the son decided to have a proper ceremony for his father. That's where we came in. Since he was a big part of the city's history, the city was going to honor him with a full military funeral at the oldest cemetery in the city.

There are a number of dignitaries buried there including a President of the United States.

We all gathered at the Justice Center and were bused to the cemetery about 15 miles from downtown. Gathered there were the Mayor, Safety Director, Chief of Police, Marching Unit, Rifle Squad and The Pipes and Drums.

After we performed our part of the ceremony, the lieutenant from Ports and Harbor took the urn and got into a row boat and rowed out to the middle of a small lake where the ashes were dispersed with a 21 gun salute. There was no burial. Weird but true.

CHAPTER 12

MEETING WITH DIGNITARIES

Ronald Reagan our 40th President

I met Ronald Reagan in 1980 when he was running for president for the first time. I had to admire the man because he was 69 years old at that time. He was in office for eight years which meant he was in his late 70's when he left office. This picture is one of my favorite possessions.

Over the years I had the good fortune to meet many V.I.P.s. In S.W.A.T. we had to guard any president or vice president, or even the presidential candidate. Also we had several big name entertainers and other celebrities. While in the aviation unit, we did presidential motorcades and escorts and finally in the motorcycle unit we did much of the same thing. This was over a span of more than 20 years.

The first president I met was Jimmy Carter and his wife Rosalyn. They were staying at a downtown hotel, and we were detailed along with the Secret Service to guarding them over night and the next morning. I have to tell you they were real folks from the south. The first night Mrs. Carter was sitting out in the hallway of the hotel with her feet up on a chair talking to the police officers and Secret Service agents just like regular folks.

Vice President Walter Mondale at the airport for a quick speech downtown. We were his assigned body guards.

Henry Kissinger came to town for an apparent important meeting, and we had security at the hotel. Then after the meeting he came out the back door and thanked all of the officers and took pictures with us.

Henry Kissinger meeting with us behind the
Downtown Hotel

During those years I was privileged to meet Teddy Kennedy, Bob Hope, Hillary Clinton, Al Gore and many others. I feel very grateful for the opportunity to meet so many of these national leaders over the years. Most people never get the chance to meet the President of the United States of America, and I met and had my picture taken with several.

Teddy Kennedy at Burke Lakefront Airport (BKL)

To Sgt. Kennith Albright
With best wishes,

CHAPTER 13

MOTORCYCLE UNIT
1997 -1999

Getting To Know My New Job

I was transferred to the motorcycle unit in November of 1997. I had always thought that I would retire from the aviation Unit, but things didn't work out that way. Now I had absolutely no experience in the traffic unit in the police department, but from day one I had always wanted to be in this unit. This was the very first transfer request that I made back in the 1971. Now 26 years late, here I was. The only problem that I could see was that I was 53 years old and hadn't ridden a motorcycle in over twenty years. Most guys my age were leaving the unit because of the physical stress of riding and especially testing every year. Tests were done in the springtime and every member had to pass this test before they were authorized to ride for the season. My age and lack of riding experience were going to be a challenge. I'm always up for challenges but like my hero Clint Eastwood in Dirty Harry said, "A man has got to know his limitations," and that's something I really try to live by.

Motorcycle Assigned 1998

From November until March I was getting my feet wet by getting the feel of what my duties were. I still had to work two shifts which is by far better than working three like other places in the department. I was one of six sergeants in the unit that was run by the lieutenant. This lieutenant is a story in itself. We would have two sergeants work each shift for the controllers and one for the motorcycle unit officers.

My day started at 6:00 A.M. I would hold roll call at 6:30 A.M. In the unit we had about 60 traffic controllers who are civilians. Their only duties were to direct traffic during rush hour and at special events. After rush hour, they gave out parking tickets and towed illegally parked cars. As their supervisor, my job was to monitor their activities and assist them whenever they had a problem. I had about 20 people to watch while the motorcycle sergeants were only responsible for a dozen or so. Plus they're working with police officers as opposed to me working with civilians which can really stretch your patience. The new sergeants would get the traffic controllers as opposed to the motorcycle officers.

This was a brand new experience for me. I never supervised non-police officers before, and they had their own rules and union that they work from. For the first couple of months I worked with another sergeant that had been in the unit for a number of years and had worked with these controllers the whole time so he knew how to handle them, or so I thought.

Motorcycle Training

In March we started our motorcycle training at a park on the west side of the city. Each and every officer is required to pass a test in order to ride the motorcycle for the season. This is from the Traffic Commissioner down to the patrolmen. Now with most of these guys it's no big deal because they have been doing it for so many years. However, I noticed this one officer was having a little trouble passing. He'd been in the unit as far back as I can remember. The reason that he was having a problem was because he was getting older and couldn't handle the grueling events required. When I found out that he was my age, I figured that if he couldn't pass, there was little chance for me.

There are 10 different events that we had to complete and each one was as hard if not even harder than the previous. Basically it was control of the motorcycle when riding at very slow speeds and doing nothing but tight turns. To accomplish these maneuvers you need to have a feel for the clutch and let it out partially. Another event was high speed braking where we would ride up to 60 M.P.H. and lock the rear brake to a stop to feel what happens to the bike. Another event was to grab the front brake and squeeze as hard as possible to show that it will not lock up like most people believe. The real trick was high speed braking without stopping and then going into a rodeo course of traffic cones. Those who get through this training will know how to ride safely with confidence.

I was so rusty that after the first couple of days, I had serious doubts that I would ever be able to get through the testing. In March it was so cold that my fingers went numb. The cold made it difficult to concentrate on riding. After a week or so, I was graciously allowed to ride on the street to get the feel of the bike, so that the next training period I was a little more comfortable and did better. After several more weeks of frustration, I finally got through the course and passed the test. Hallelujah! Now I was a full-fledged member of the Cleveland Police Motorcycle Unit.

One great thing about riding downtown in traffic during special events or rush hour when the traffic is heavy is that we are able to get around a lot easier because of the size of the bike. Believe me that comes in handy when someone needs your assistance now!

An Official Motorcycle Officer

Our lieutenant had been in the unit for a long time when I got there. I was just another sergeant in the unit. The longer I was there I could see a pattern emerging. The only way I could describe it was the lieutenant was immature. He would pick on various people and just torment them for no apparent reason other than it gave him pleasure. You were either one of his boys that hung around together after work drinking and carousing or you were someone to harass. He loved to pit one group against another and sit back and watch the fun. He would give his boys extra overtime and other benefits that the traffic unit got. I just tried to stay neutral and do my job. The traffic controllers hated him and I do mean hated. The worst case scenario an immature person with authority.

Taking Over As O.I.C. (Officer-in-Charge)

Eventually the traffic coordinator retired and the good lieutenant wanted that job as he would be a step closer to the Traffic Commissioner's job which is what he really wanted. When he left the motorcycle unit and I was going to retire within the year, I figured it can't be all that bad so I volunteered to take over the job of Officer-In-Charge of the Motorcycle Unit. It wouldn't be such a bad gig because I would get to make all of the decisions. All of the responsibilities which were massive came along too. My only stipulation was that I alone would run the unit. I wanted no outside interference. This was mostly because of the lieutenant that left. He just loved to stick his nose in places that he shouldn't and start trouble. I even typed up a report stating such and had all the members of the unit sign and kept a copy. I knew he would still want to run the unit during different events and try to take over like he was still in charge. In my report I just stated to my people that if any supervisor other than your immediate one wants to give you an order, respectfully advise them to contact your boss. I felt that if I didn't take charge, there would be confusion because as the old saying goes, "The right hand doesn't know what the left hand is doing." So I took over the motorcycle unit for the last 10 months on the job. It was another dream come true for me. Like I said before, I had wanted to be in the motorcycle unit from day one and here I was the officer in charge. The good Lord does care about our lives.

I had about 60 civilian traffic controllers and about 30 officers under my command. Normally, a minimum of six sergeants would handle this many people but over the next couple of months we lost all but two. I was making a lot of over time up until now being so shorthanded. I was doubling my pay every pay period which amounted to 80 hours of O.T. every two weeks.

For take home money that's not so great because the government will eat you alive, but for retirement it's great because pension is calculated based on the highest three years. Putting in that many hours started to take its toll. After so much time spent at work I had absolutely no other kind of life. Up until coming to this unit I had never had any dealings with non-police personnel. This was a new experience for me, and it was something that I had to get used to.

On one occasion all of the traffic lights went out due to a power failure. Most of the major intersections were without traffic lights, and I could just picture the accidents that were about to happen. I called for all of the controllers that were working to meet me at a specified location. After several minutes I got no response. As I was driving down the street, I noticed a couple of the controllers' cars parked in front of a hotel. I parked and went inside the restaurant and found six of them just sitting there waiting for their lunch. Normally I'm pretty even tempered, but I do have a switch that can be thrown and this did it. When I asked them what was going on they said that they had just ordered lunch and after lunch they would respond. I almost lost control of myself. I could not believe what I was hearing. I had been in the Army for three years and on the police department for the last 28 years and was pretty spoiled about having people respond to an order immediately without question or delay. I told the waitress to cancel the order and told them in no uncertain terms that if they weren't outside in two minutes, they would all go up on charges. I don't remember ever being that angry except with my kids.

Well they made it out, and I posted one to each intersection without any further problem, but from then on I was known as a real hard ass.

The first full year that I was in the unit we had seven motorcycle accidents. They were mostly minor, but still that just shows you how dangerous riding a motorcycle can be. You have two wheels under you with nothing else surrounding you for protection. One day I was riding around downtown during an event. The traffic was fairly heavy but nothing unusual. I was going east on Euclid

190

Avenue just crossing East 9th Street when I noticed another officer behind me coming up in the same direction. He wasn't to East 9th Street yet but there's an alley about half a block away. All of a sudden a female driver came flying out of the alley, struck the officer, and knocked him to the ground. She just came barreling out of the alley without looking. Fortunately, there were no pedestrians on the sidewalk at the time because if there were, she probably would have either killed them or seriously injured them. I turned around and went back to check on the motorcycle officer. He was OK, but there was enough damage to the bike that it had to be towed. Most of the time the accidents were minor because most patrolling was done on city streets where we travelled at relatively slow speeds.

CHAPTER 14

New Adventure – RETIREMENT!

November 12, 1999

Herding cattle in Idaho in the summer

I retired from the police department in November of 1999. I had 30 years and one month on the job. The pension system is set up so that full benefits are calculated at 72 percent after 33 years of service, and they take your highest three years. I had 30 years which would have given me about 70 percent. If you had military service or time in another department, you were able to buy that time to go along with city time. So that's what I did. I bought three years of my military time which gave me my max pension of 72 percent.

We bought a house in Fairview Park after retiring using the money I received from the city for my overtime and sick time that I hadn't used. We lived there for a couple of years but decided to move south to the Atlanta, Georgia area where the winters are not as bad and where we had family. As it turned out my youngest son moved down about six months before we did. We bought a house that was still under construction and stayed with my sister for a couple of weeks until it was finished. My retirement has gone very well most of the time.

Alaskan Snow Blower... Minus 20 today

Heart Attack

Then in June of 2004 I woke up in the middle of the night with your classic chest pains. It was a pretty hard ache on the left side of my chest. I got up and tried to walk it off thinking that it was heart burn or something, but after about 20 minutes I started to realize that it might actually be a heart attack. Knowing that my wife can't handle any type of pressure, I got her up and told her to call an ambulance. I didn't trust her behind the wheel of a car when she's nervous and upset. The fire rescue arrived in just a few minutes, and the first thing that they did was to give me a nitro pill. They took me to the nearest hospital which was about 20 minutes away.

When I arrived at the hospital, they rushed me into the emergency room and started to give me all of the normal tests to see if I was having a heart attack. After a few hours the results were back, and it was determined that at least one of the main arteries was 95 percent closed. I was admitted immediately. This was on a Friday, and they were planning on giving me the dye test to determine exactly what was going on. Monday morning they checked again and decided that they couldn't do the dye test because of the closed artery. Instead they sent me to Piedmont Hospital in downtown Atlanta where they do procedures relating to the heart. I waited all day and finally rode in the back of the ambulance in a torrential rain to Piedmont Hospital which took quite a while.

Finally, we arrived and right away they prepared me for the coronary angiography. The test involves inserting a scope into the groin and moving slowly up into the heart.

After the procedure was done and I was wheeled back to a room, I was finally told that there was a blood clot in my artery, and when it broke loose the artery spasm closed to about 95 percent. When they went in, the doctor shot some nitro directly into the heart and it miraculously opened completely. They didn't have to do anything more.

Now again this was all by chance, so if this was chance then I'm either one of the luckiest guys around or The Good Lord still had His hand on my life!

Off The Mountain

2012 Motorcycle accident, Pine Mountain, Georgia

I was back in good health and back in the saddle so to speak and on one sunny Saturday morning the Music Minister and I decided to take a motorcycle ride. We had been on several rides at this point in my retirement. We usually would ride the back roads south of Senoia, Georgia, and down to Pine Mountain, where there are a lot of winding roads going up and down the mountain. The ride would usually last anywhere from two to four hours. The motorcycle that I was riding was a Yamaha Silverado Roadstar. I had it for a couple of years at this point and put on several thousand miles. By now I was pretty comfortable riding it.

We had just stopped for lunch and got back on the road. Jon led the way as he knew where we were going. I was still learning my way around the area. This is the area where F.D.R. had his house called the Little White House in Warm Springs, Georgia. As we started the ride I was behind Jon, but he started to pull away. So I increased my speed to catch up and as I started into a fairly steep left curve my back tire slipped. That small slip was enough to throw me off the turn. I was going fairly fast at the time and in that split second, I was off the road going through small trees and shrubbery. After that I don't really remember what happened until I was down at the bottom of a 10 foot cliff with the motorcycle lying on top of me. This model motorcycle weighed about 800 pounds. My arms were pinned at my side, and the bike was on my chest. I attempted to move, but the weight was so heavy that I was completely immovable. I smelled gasoline coming from the gas tank leaking on the ground around me.

As I took inventory of my situation, I knew that Jon would not know where I was because I was so far off the road, and there was no indication of where I went off. It was up to me to get myself free from under the bike. I wasn't hurting too badly, except for the weight of the bike on my chest. I didn't have any broken bones so far as I could tell when I attempted to move. I knew that I was in a very bad situation and that I just had to get out by myself. I started to wiggle my body, struggling to pull myself out from under the bike. As I struggled, I started to move forward just a little.I worked at it until I finally got my arms free, and then I was able to pull the rest of my body out.

The first thing I did was to check on the condition of the motorcycle to see if it was drivable. It started right up when I hit the starter button. I put it in gear and attempted to climb up the cliff, but it was too steep and I was unable get more than a couple of feet. After several tries I climbed up and over until I got to the road. When I got to the top, I looked around and there was no traffic and no Jon. I lost my cell phone, so there was no way that I could contact anyone.

My chest was hurting and I didn't know if I had broken any bones. Also I had several cuts where small trees and limbs had cut my hands as I went over the cliff.

Finally, after what seemed like a life time, I saw Jon coming back from the opposite way we had come. Apparently, he had ridden several more miles before he realized that I wasn't behind him. When the dust settled, he called for a tow and gave them our location per the mile marker. It only took about a half hour for the tow truck to arrive. The driver hooked the chain to the front of the bike and pulled it to the top. That's when we noticed the front rim, tire and forks were twisted and bent. There would be no way I could drive it.

When I arrived home in the tow truck, I called the insurance company and notified them of the accident. They said that they would have someone out Monday morning. True to their word an adjuster arrived first thing Monday. After looking over the motorcycle, he recommended a total loss. A short time later the insurance company paid off my complete loan which was a blessing in itself. I went to the doctor after a couple of days just to check out my chest to see if in fact anything was broken. The doctor checked me out, and I had x-rays which showed everything was good. My chest was sore for a couple of weeks but I had no other injuries which was another blessing. This could have been my last story. Actually it is... for this book.

Live your life in Thanksgiving to the Lord. You'll be better for it.
Have a Happy Retirement.

Some advice for you that are planning to retire - Do Stuff!
And, in your life,
"Don't die doin' something stupid."

Romans 13:1-5

Submission to the Authorities:

1. *Everyone must submit himself to the governing authorities, for there is no authority except that which God has established. The authorities that exist have been established by God.*

2. *Consequently, he who rebels against the authority is rebelling against what God has instituted and those who do so will bring judgment on themselves.*

3. *For rulers hold no terror for those who do right but for those who do wrong. Do you want to be free from fear of the one in authority? Then do what is right and he will commend you.*

4. *For he is God's servant to do you good. But if you do wrong, be afraid, for he does not bear the sword for nothing. He is God's servant, an agent of wrath to bring punishment on the wrongdoer.*

5. *Therefore, it is necessary to submit to the authorities, not only because of possible punishment but also because of conscience.*

Special Remembrance and Dedication to the Families of the 18 Officers whose lives were lost during my 30 year Career.

Detective Robert James Clark, II
EOW: Wednesday, July 1, 1998   Cause: Gunfire

Patrol Officer Hilary S. Cudnik
EOW: Monday, December 30, 1996   Cause: Gunfire

Patrolman Thomas J. Smith
EOW: Tuesday, March 9, 1993   Cause: Gunfire

Patrolman Ernest Cecil Holbert
EOW: Tuesday, October 27, 1987   Cause: Gunfire

Patrolman Stephen M. Kovach
EOW: Sunday, March 11, 1984   Cause: Gunfire

Patrolman Benjamin F. Grair, Jr.
EOW: Friday, August 5, 1983   Cause: Gunfire

Police Officer Anthony Jerome Johnson
EOW: Wednesday, October 21, 1981   Cause: Gunfire

Officer Desmond Sherry
EOW: Thursday, July 3, 1980   Cause: Gunfire

Detective George Zicarelli
EOW: Monday, September 17, 1979   Cause: Gunfire

Patrolman John L. Hubbell
EOW: Monday, June 4, 1979   Cause: Gunfire

Patrolman John S. Reese
EOW: Thursday, September 2, 1976   Cause: Gunfire

Captain Jerome C. Poelking
EOW: Monday, December 8, 1975 Cause: Duty related illness

Patrolman Edward W. Murray, Jr.
EOW: Wednesday, July 2, 1975   Cause: Gunfire

Patrolman William Nathan Shapiro
EOW: Friday, April 26, 1974   Cause: Gunfire

Patrolman Frederick D. Vacha
EOW: Wednesday, June 20, 1973   Cause: Gunfire

Patrolman William Nagy
EOW: Friday, May 14, 1971   Cause: Gunfire

Patrolman Tom Sam Hakaim

EOW: Saturday, April 3, 1971   Cause: Gunfire

Patrolman Joseph Phillip Tracz, Jr.

EOW: Monday, September 28, 1970   Cause: Gunfire

MEET THE AUTHOR

I certainly hope you've enjoyed the book. If so, please leave a short review with Amazon.com.

Feel free to join me on FaceBook - "One Cop's Story."

Perhaps if you were an officer during the period you'd like to leave your story or discuss an event. I look forward to it.

Best Regards,

Ken D. Albright, Sgt Retired.

EPILOGUE

I had the good fortune to be raised by a Godly mother who was widowed and providing for four children. We lived in one of the projects in a Cleveland suburb. She worked hard and she prayed for her children on a daily basis. At some point a new man entered our lives and soon became our stepdad.

I remember back when I was living at home, the pastor and deacon from the local church would come over to visit with my mother. My stepdad and I would see them coming and run into the garage and stay there until they left. We didn't want to hear anything about their religion or beliefs. We just figured they were there to visit with my mom anyway, but in reality they had come to tell my dad and me about Jesus. I thank God that this same deacon led my dad to Jesus 18 years later just before his death. If it wasn't for faithful workers like this man, my sweet dad wouldn't be with the Lord today. One day I'll get to see him again.

I graduated from high school in 1963 by the skin of my teeth. All through school I made the bare minimum to pass. I never got the connection between studying, doing homework, and getting good grades. I figured that it came by osmosis. The only goal that I had during school was to get out. I didn't participate in extracurricular activities and wasn't considered one of the popular jocks. I had a few good friends I hung out with, and we did practically everything together. Unfortunately, we shared the same goals, too.

After graduating I worked at minimum wage jobs with no goal or motivation to do anything with my life. So it was good that in February of 1965 I got my draft notice. If anything would get a young man's mind thinking about his future, it was the letter of notice saying you've been drafted. I knew that I didn't want to be in the infantry and the only other option was to join which meant going an extra year. Instead of two years I would have to go for three years. I figured what the heck, I wasn't doing anything here and I could get trained for a good job that I could pursue when I got out. I went in to the recruiter's office and signed all the documents in triplicate and selected the field of electronics. The school was in New Jersey just 40 miles south of New York City.

I took my basic training at Fort Knox, Kentucky, and three months later started electronic training at Fort Monmouth, New Jersey. There I spent the next eight months going to school during the week and partying in New York on the weekends. I did the exact same thing there that I did in high school hoping to learn through osmosis. I never studied and barely made it through. From there I was shipped out to Ft. Lewis Washington near Seattle. I traveled by train. It took us three days to get there. After three weeks I volunteered to go to the Dominican Republic. A revolt had broken out in major parts of the capital Santa Domingo in 1965, and in order to quell the situation, the U.S. (the policemen of the world I guess) sent in troops. I was there for six months in 1966. When we pulled out, our troops had been there for a total of a year and a half.

We took an LST transport back to the states and after three days at sea we landed in North Carolina and then were transported to Fort Bragg. I spent two weeks there and then back to Fort Lewis.

After three more weeks at Lewis I volunteered to go TDY to Germany. Since I was in electronics and the European headquarters was moving from Paris to Stuttgart, Germany, we were sent to set up temporary communications until they were permanently situated. Like everything else up to this point, I just bluffed my way through. I never really studied, so I really had no idea of what I was doing. What I was learning, however, was that it's harder to bluff your way than it would've been to study and learn.

During this time period the U.S. armed forces were building up strength in Vietnam. From 1965 until 1968 the ground forces went from 50,000 troops to 500,000. Everyone that went into the military could expect to go to Nam. Probably 90 percent of my graduating class from Fort Monmouth went. At the time I thought I was just lucky that I was not sent to Vietnam. Now I know that the Lord was there guiding my life unbeknownst to me. By the war's end more than 58,000 young American boys had been killed in action, and who knows how many more were wounded or maimed. Thousands more saw so much killing that they would never be the same again without God's Grace on them.

When I got back from Germany, I had 10 months left on my tour of duty. It was required to have at least 12 months or more to go to Vietnam. So I spent my last 10 months stateside at an electronic military post that the U.S. Calvary used for fighting Indians in the 1800's. Fort Huachuca was in the middle of the desert just 15 miles north of the Mexican border. The closest large city was Tucson 70 miles northwest of the fort. I immediately went home and bought a car so I had transportation. I couldn't believe that the Army would put me out in nowhere land for 10 months. At 23 years of age it was pure torture. After a while I started visiting different areas in the state like Tombstone, Bisbee and Nogales and fell in love with the cowboy atmosphere. I always knew that I was a cowboy at heart. I have been back several times since I got out of the Army. I even took Ruth there and she too fell in love with the state.

After the Army I moved back home and got a job with ADT Alarm Company. I was married five months later to my sister's husband's sister. It's not as confusing as it sounds. My sister Judy married Harry and I married his sister, Ruth.

I accepted the Lord back in the mid 1970's after my wife had been attending church for some time. She's the one who really guided me to start going to church and hearing the Word of God. We had a growing family at the time and felt our kids needed the type of foundation that only a good Christian church could help us provide. We had become pretty active in our church, and it wasn't long before I was nominated as a Deacon while my wife taught Sunday School and ran the bus ministry. We also decided to send our boys to a Christian school that had just started up. They were looking for a bus driver; we figured it would help pay the tuition. So, Ruth would get up at the crack of dawn and get the boys ready and make the rounds picking up the other children from our suburb and the surrounding area near downtown where the school was located. She would make the drive again every day for the return trip home. She did this for a few years, and it wouldn't have been too bad if the little school van was in better condition. When it rained I would need to go start the bus by crawling underneath and jumping the solenoid, a trick I soon taught my wife. Admittedly, we thanked God when a teen age boy took the corner of our street too quickly and hit the back of the little van, shoving it into our closed garage door. There were no injuries other than to his pride as he left the scene and his father brought him back. Needless to say, our little van was finally replaced.

After several years of this, the stress and strain of all we had taken on began to really wear on us. I was becoming burnt out mainly from the responsibilities of being a Deacon at such an early time in my Christian walk. I was too new in the faith to realize all the demands of the position. I slowly started to drift away from all church activity and after moving to a new community and changing churches. It was easy to just stop going.

"When you fail to study God's Word you stop growing.
When you cease to grow spiritually you start deteriorating
immediately.
When you stop climbing you start slipping.
You can never arrive spiritually in this life. There is always a
higher plateau to be reached."

This was where I was in my life. I had stopped growing and started slipping and once you start down that road, with our sinful nature, it's very easy to fall into sin.

The temptations on the police department are far greater than those in other professions. There are so many vices and temptations out there that unless you are walking close to the Lord, you can easily slide right into them. Every aspect of our lives was in trouble. We started to have problems in our marriage, and we only went to church once in a while. Once that happens it's nearly impossible to recover. We were just existing and not really living the life that the Lord had for us.

In the late 1990's we had taken custody of our oldest grandson for a time to help his parents who were having problems of their own. We started attending a church that we thought would help us as a couple and make sure that our grandson was being taught the Word of God. I knew that we needed God in our lives if we were to have the type of marriage God intended. We signed up for a twelve week course that was being offered by the church and slowly started getting our lives back together. The closer we got to God, the closer our marriage became.

I retired from the police department in November of 1999. We moved to a Cleveland suburb and my wife started working part time. After a couple of winters with all the snow and cold we decided to move down to Georgia where my sister had been living for the last 30 years.

We really felt we had found our long lost home down here. The small town we relocated to felt like "Mayberry U.S.A." After working in a large city all of my life this laid back life style was exactly what we needed. We still had to find a home church in the area and attended several without really feeling like this was where the Lord wanted us to be.

During the time my wife had been working at a lawyer's office for a couple of years.

One day she was let go because the lawyer's wife retired from her regular job and would work for her husband in Ruth's place. That afternoon she was getting her hair done when the hairdresser mentioned that the local church was looking for a secretary. The next day Ruth applied for the position and was hired immediately as a fill in while their temp secretary was on vacation. As we were still looking for a home church and Ruth had gotten to know the pastor and his beliefs, we decided to try this one. It was like walking into your own home after many years. The people were friendly and made us feel welcome. Top that with the fearless preaching of the Word of God, and we knew without a shadow of doubt that God led us there.

After becoming members we became involved in many of the activities and were finally, once again, on our way to becoming what the Lord planned for us. We were working and praising the Lord with one another and enjoying the fellowship of a family. There is no greater feeling in the world because this is what God our Father intended for us. I'm a stay-at-home husband who cleans the house, does the dishes and makes lunch and dinner. And as for our marriage, it's the best that it's ever been. The Lord is in the business of doing the impossible.

That's what it took to advance from merely existing to living. Despite all the times that I was spared, I never really put it all together. That shows you how blind we can be. After coming to the brink of death eight to ten times you start to wonder: What does the Lord Almighty want with me? What does He want me for? Those questions aren't for us to worry about. Our job as Christians is to turn over all to Christ Jesus. He'll take care of the rest.

I'm at the point in life now where I can look back and see all that God has done in my life. It humbles me so that there is no way that I can possibly do enough to pay Him back. The only thing that I want to do now is to turn my life over to Him and let Him use me for His glory.

I want to do all that the Lord has for me. So far, I've become an ordained deacon, taught adult Sunday school classes and had the privilege to work with the AWANAs. I now teach 3 and 4 year olds through Mission Friends on Wednesday nights, sing in the choir, and serve as the Facilities Coordinator.

The only thing that the Lord asks of any of His children is to just be available for Him and to use the "Gifts" that He has given each one of us.

There is only one way to get into Heaven!

John 14:6 [6] Jesus answered, "I am the way and the truth and the life. No one comes to the Father except through me."

God makes it easy for anyone to be saved from eternal damnation. You cannot work your way in, or be good enough, or by living a good life.

Romans 3:10

[10] As it is written: There is no one righteous, not even one.

Romans 3:23

[23] For all have sinned and fall short of the glory of God.

Romans 6:23

[23] For the wages of sin is death, but the gift of God is eternal life in Christ Jesus our Lord.

Romans 5:8

[8] But God demonstrates his own love for us in this: While we were still sinners, Christ died for us.

Romans 10:9

[9] If you declare with your mouth, "Jesus is Lord," and believe in your heart that God raised him from the dead, you will be saved.

Romans 10:13

[13] For, Everyone who calls on the name of the Lord will be saved.

The Lord does not want to see anyone go to Hell, but we all have freewill to decide for ourselves. He came to save the lost. Salvation is a free gift for anyone to accept, but it's like receiving any gift, we first have to accept it before it's ours.

God Bless.

217